STORIES OF A

MANCHESTER STREET

STORIES OF A

MANCHESTER STREET

Phil Barton & Elaine Bishop

This book has been published with the support of

First published 2019

The History Press
The Mill, Brimscombe Port
Stroud, Gloucestershire, GL5 2QG
www.thehistorypress.co.uk

British Library Cataloguing in Publication Data.
A catalogue record for this book is available from the British Library.

ISBN 978 0 7509 9047 9

Typesetting and origination by The History Press
Printed in Great Britain

Patterned backgrounds © Rawpixel.com - Freepik.com

Contents

Introduction

⟫◦⟪

Rusholme, located south of Manchester city centre, is typical of many English post-industrial cities. A village in the countryside as recently as the 1830s, it was rapidly engulfed as Manchester industrialised and its population grew. Initially a development of grand houses for the newly wealthy of Manchester, it was later surrounded by terraced workers' housing before further infill housing between 1900 and the 1960s. Today it is in the grip of a further development boom focused on the three universities and the major hospitals immediately to the north.

Our street was speculatively built on fields first sold in 1836 and then sold on in 1905 and was almost completely occupied by the time of the 1911 census.

In 2011 residents held a centenary party for our street, and Harry Spooner, a neighbour, researched the original occupancy of the houses. He found a print-out of the 1911 Census occupants listed for each house which we displayed on our front gateposts. At the party the initial idea for *Stories from a Manchester Street* was born and two years later, in November 2013, the first household interview took place. Since then we have interviewed most of the households and have taken a photograph of residents in front of their homes. With their agreement, these interviews and portraits have been included in this book.

We found that residents were born in at least eighteen countries from every continent except Australasia and South America. People of Muslim, Hindu, Catholic, Anglican, Jewish, Buddhist, non-conformist Christian and of no faith, along with the international congregation of the New Apostolic Church, live happily together in harmony. The street is home to people in a wide range of occupations, and none.

The interviews tell the stories of journeys from Somalia and from rural Ireland, of conscientious objection and refugees fleeing the Second World War, of Partition in India, Pakistan and Bangladesh and of meetings leading to lifetime partnerships at university, in communities of origin, in the workplace and on a film set. They tell of

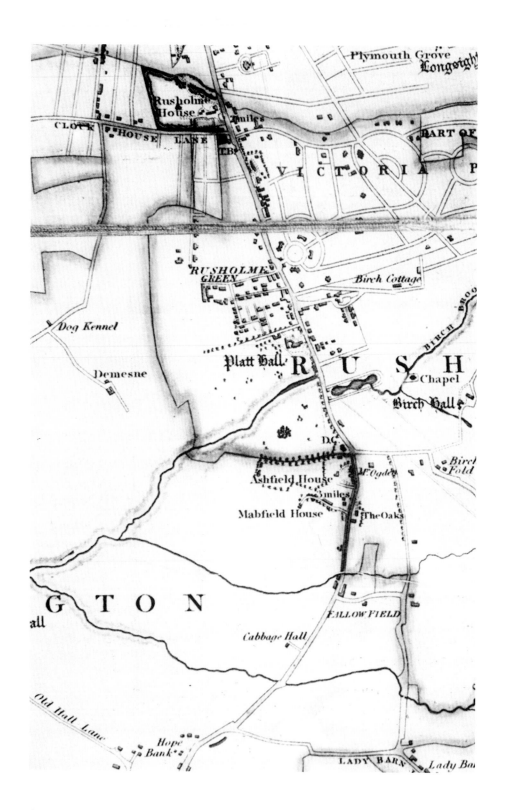

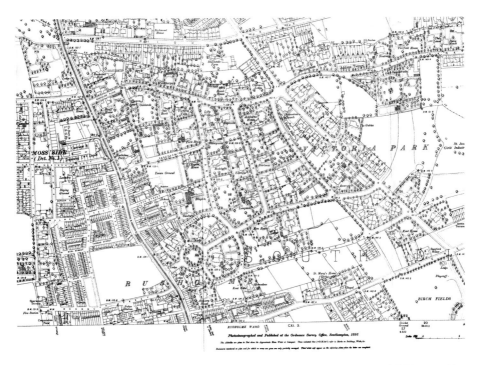

Rusholme in 1838 (left) and in 1889, from Johnson's Map of Manchester and OS Lancashire sheet 104.15 respectively.

family houses and houses in multiple occupation, houses accommodating children, elderly relatives and those who are unwell. And once these stories were collected and read out to neighbours, the cultural melting pot that is our street became visible and our community stronger.

The stories in this book have emerged from a decade of community action following the establishment of our residents' group and communal activities ranging from street tree planting to street parties and fundraising for flood victims in Pakistan to regular clean-ups. Neighbours have read their stories together, produced a primary-school project book based on this work and hosted an academic workshop with the University of Manchester. The photographs were shown at an open day at Victoria Baths – a fine building contemporaneous with our street – which won the first BBC Restoration series and is being restored by a trust.

We have worked closely with our local councillors who have facilitated funding and connections with Manchester City Council, demonstrating the importance of support to enable communities to thrive. This could be the story of any street in our inner cities. It shows a picture far removed from the headlines and divisive politics of our times. It shows how people of goodwill can find common

Biochemist
SchoolStudent
CharityWorker Priest
SalesManager
Construction
Teacher Physiotherapist Lecturer
Pharmacist Housewife
Catering
Student
TradesUnionist Gardener ITManager
Musician CompanyDirector
Midwife Translator Unemployed
ArtsAdministrator
SocialWorker
RetailSales TaxiDriver Retired
Accountant
UnderSchoolAge

Above: Word map of the reported occupations on the street.

Left: Rashid with his father in Glasgow during the 1970s when he was working on market stalls. (*Photo courtesy of Rashid*)

cause in a respectful, supportive and vibrant community, working together to tackle problems, whether it is litter and rubbish in the streets or over-development by landlords or, on a wider canvas, Manchester's communal response to the Arena bombing in 2017.

Between the two of us we have lived on our street for fifty-six years. We would like to thank our neighbours and friends for their consistent enthusiasm for this project. We hope that readers will take as much from these rich and varied stories as we have – and that

The street in the early 1970s (*Photo: Manchester Libraries & Archives*) and as it is today. The arrows, the street tree in the foreground, the alley gates, the Christmas tree and the community garden (out of shot to the left) have all been achieved by residents acting together in the past ten years.

in 2111 residents in our street will know more about those living in our homes a hundred years ago than we do about those who lived here in 1911.

Phil Barton & Elaine Bishop
February 2019

Note on the methodology

The interviews were carried out between November 2013 and September 2018. The book contains the stories of the households at the time of the interview taking place. In some cases they have since moved on. Some of the houses on the street are empty; some whole households– and some residents within the households featured – did not wish to be interviewed. In all cases the interviewees were given the opportunity to correct or amend the story they told us before it was included in this book. The group portraits were taken by arrangement and in the available natural light. They have not been digitally manipulated.

Judith and Ron

Judith and Ron have lived on the street since 1975

Judith and Ron

Judith's Journey

I was born in Withington in Manchester in 1937. Both my parents were civil servants. They married late in life so my sister and I were much loved and cosseted 'miracle babies'. After attending Manchester High School for Girls I went to Kings' College where I studied Classics, and after graduation, in 1958, I stayed in London and went to work at Peckham Manor School as a general form teacher. I had tried out all sorts of possible careers as Saturday jobs and finally decided that teaching was for me. The school was a newly formed comprehensive amalgamating several small secondary and all-age schools but when I arrived on my first day, my classroom had no furniture. I found a chair somewhere and the children sat on the floor for several weeks! We got by through mental arithmetic, storytelling and me playing the violin.

My future husband, Ron, was also a teacher at the school, arriving the year after I did. He organised the junior rugby team, most of whom belonged to my class. These boys persuaded me to support them on Saturday matches so I often found myself sitting next to Ron on the rugby bus. After that, we became an 'item' and in 1960 we married.

I had stopped working when we had our first child, and when I was ready to start again I wrote to my old high school for a 'testimonial' which I intended to use to get another job. They wrote back saying they had a position in the Classics Department, and to come back to them. We moved to Manchester in 1961. It was good being near my mum and my sister and Ron liked Manchester and was happy to come back, too. He found a job in Salford teaching maths and we moved into a flat in Withington where we stayed for a year while saving for a house. In 1962 we bought a house in Rusholme. We had thirteen happy years there with our four children. But during the last year, my mother became ill and moved in with us and stayed until she died. It was painful and took some of the shine off the house and I thought it would be good to move somewhere else after that. This house has been my home for thirty-eight years.

Ron's Journey

I was born in 1936 in Goole, Yorkshire, and was an only child. My father worked in various jobs as an 'electrician's mate', including a spell as a projectionist at the local cinema. During my childhood my mother didn't work but was very involved in volunteering and was a leading light in the Women's Royal Volunteer Service. She was a very good cook, and after I left home to go to Hull University she ran a canteen at British Rail. Hull University was then in its early days, with only 600 students. I studied mathematics. After graduation I contacted London County Council to see if there were any teaching vacancies. I got an instant response from Peckham Manor Comprehensive to come for an interview and started work there almost immediately.

After we had started our family and moved back to Manchester I called into the Education Department to see about getting a job. They had no vacancies for maths teachers so they sent me across the Irwell to Chapel Street and I began teaching in Salford.

Judith and Ron

We had made many friends in the community and one family, who lived around the corner, had bought this house with a bank loan. They had intended to swap it for a mortgage but in those days you couldn't swap. With oil crises and three-day weeks, interest rates soon went sky high, up to 17 per cent. They were in dire financial straits. We loved the house and easily got a mortgage so we decided to swap houses and moved here in 1975. We went out to the Tandoori Kitchen for a meal with our friends and while we were there, the pantechnicon brought our furniture here and returned to our old house with theirs. We have been here thirty-eight years now. Our four children came with us, the oldest 15 and the youngest 8. The kids loved it here, playing in the grounds of the old High School.

It took us a while to get to know people on the street because we were busy with the children and both of us working. At that time, the street was full of boarding houses; our house was known as 'Flatlet House'. We took in lodgers too and had students staying with us for several years. The street has always been full of foreigners and when we moved in there were many Germans and East Europeans here, including Czechs, Poles and Hungarians; No. 2 was a house of ill repute! The first long-term resident we met was Eric Voigt, the violin maker, who had been living in the house across the street since 1948. And we knew Kathleen Donnelly and two of her children, who all had houses on the street, because they were also our close neighbours before. Later we connected with fellow allotment holders and Labour Party members.

It is a much more sociable street these days, especially since the formation of our new Residents' Association in 2009, and there are many families with children of similar ages who all know each other through school and local playgroups.

We are now about to do another house swap, buying our daughter's smaller house in Urmston while our son and grandson take our place here. But we are keeping a bedroom for our use so we aren't really leaving yet!

RESIDENTS IN 1911

BELL, Robert
Born: 1868
Barrow in Furness, Lancashire
Occupation: Assistant Solicitor
to Manchester Corporation

BELL, Edith Louisa
Born: 1867
Edinburgh, Midlothian
Occupation: Wife

NEEDHAM, Maud, Ellen
Born: 1888
Taddington, Derbyshire
Occupation: Domestic
Housemaid

RESIDENTS IN 2014

Ron
Born: 1936
Goole, Yorkshire
Occupation: Retired
Mathematics Teacher

Judith
Born: 1937
Withington, Manchester
Occupation: Retired Classics
Teacher

Rashid and Robena

Rashid came to live on the street in 1984

Rashid (left) and Robena (third left), with members of their family
(*photo: Elaine Bishop*)

Rashid's Journey

I came to England in 1968. My father was a textile engineer and brought his family first to Huddersfield, then Oldham and finally to Glasgow, where we had an aunt living. My father wanted to see his children educated. I went to school in Glasgow, first to Kinning Park High School and then Shawlands Academy. I left school in 1970 and started working in a grocer's shop and then got a job as a knitting machine operator in Manchester City Centre. I lived in Longsight on Hamilton Road and then on Sunnybank Road. I got my driver's licence and started doing open markets from Thursday to Sunday around Glasgow until 1976. I was around 20 years old. At the same time I was also producing my own knitwear on a hand machine which I then developed into a very successful business, with a small factory based in Ardwick. I ran the business for over ten years until 1989. I bought this house in 1984. By then I had separated from my brothers and had gone out on my own. I was driving around and saw the house and fell in love with both the house and with the area. We used to pass through this neighbourhood on our way to the Curry Mile when we lived in Glasgow. I never thought I would buy a house here! In 1989, I bought business premises in the Northern Quarter near the Craft Centre, then sold it and invested in a restaurant in the Curry Mile in 1991 (The Shiraz, next to Kebabish). I had the restaurant for three years but lost it by 1994 (there was a lot of competition) and lost a lot of money, too. I managed to save the house. After that I worked four years in a knitwear factory to get back on my feet, until 1999. Now I am retired and drive a taxi from time to time.

We brought our children up in Manchester. I always told them, *'Don't do anything wrong. Don't compare yourself to others. If you have willpower you can do anything. The government here gives you the best chance.'* One of my sons is a civil engineer and architect; one is working at a takeaway, another son is head boy at Burnage High School and is planning to be a dental surgeon and hoping to go to Cambridge. He is also a very talented artist. My daughter is at Xaverian College in Manchester and wants to be a solicitor.

On living on this street

If you are a millionaire you can have bad neighbours and you are living in hell. If your neighbours are nice you are living in a palace whether you have any money or not. Our religion says that the fifty houses around you are your community and key to your happiness. We really appreciate working with our neighbours to look after the lovely garden we have all made. Even though things are tight these days, even if I won £10 million in the lottery I wouldn't leave this house.

RESIDENTS IN 1911	RESIDENTS IN 2019
TATTERSALL, George Bardsley Born: 1876 Manchester Lancashire Occupation: Head Master Elementary School	Rashid Born: 1955 Lyalleur, Province of Punjab, Pakistan Occupation: Retired and part-time Taxi Driver
TATTERSALL, Ada Born: 1872 Manchester Lancashire Occupation: Wife	Robena Born: 1964 Lyalleur, Province of Punjab, Pakistan Occupation: Housewife and Mother

Sophie, Tony and Stephen

Sophie and Tony have lived on the street since 2004; Stephen since 2014

Left to right: Tony, Stephen and Sophie

Tony's Journey

My dad was a musician and played in the big bands in the fifties. He gave it up when skiffle came in, though he continued playing on the weekends. My mum was mostly a housewife but she was very talented and made accessories for dresses, jackets, etc. Both parents were in the fire service in the war in the docks and lived in Battersea where my older sister and I grew up. I went to primary school and Sir Walter St John's Grammar School there. Battersea was still full of bombsites then. I left school after A-levels and went straight to work, applying for a post at Polydor Recording Studio in Bond Street that Mum had seen advertised. They were looking for an 'experienced sound recording engineer'. I went and said, *'I know nothing but am willing to learn.'* They hired me and I watched and learned, working for various recording studios for thirteen years. For seven of those years (1975–82) I lived in Iceland, working at Iceland's first recording studio. I was only supposed to be there for three months but stayed seven years. I loved it.

In the early 80s I was offered a job on a film as a boom operator. I had never done that before but I took to it like a duck to water. I loved working in films and drifted out of music. I initially worked with a sound recordist from Glasgow so left London in 1984 and moved to Glasgow. I lived there for more than nineteen years, working on films on location and in London and Glasgow, including *The Crying Game* and *Trainspotting*. In 2001, I met Sophie on a film, *Once upon a Time in the Midlands*, which drew me to Manchester where Sophie lived. We lived on the Burnage/Levenshulme border. I worked freelance all this time.

Sophie's Journey

I was born in London but grew up in Southwell in Nottinghamshire. I realise, looking back, what a blessed childhood it was. We moved to Nottingham when I was two and a half because my dad, who was a theatre designer, set up a course in that subject there. We stayed briefly and then moved to Southwell around 1966. My mum was also a theatre designer and skilled costumier. While we (I have a brother three years younger) were children, she didn't go out to work but took on various costume jobs which she could do from home. I went to primary school in Southwell, and then for secondary to Sibford Friends School (a Quaker boarding school in the Cotswold countryside) for five years. I did my Sixth Form in York at a Quaker school called 'The Mount'.

After York I came to Manchester. Dad had been asked to come here to be Resident Designer for the Royal Exchange. We moved up to Whaley Bridge and I applied to the Foundation in Art course at Manchester Polytechnic. It was fantastic. I was in an 'experimental' group with quite a few mature students. It was a blossoming for me not to be constrained by school and rules. I was there from 1979–80 and then went to Nottingham to do a three-year degree course in theatre design. From there I got work pretty quickly on small-scale pieces of theatre and was even employed by one of my tutors. My big break came through my Dad, when the wardrobe mistress from the Royal Exchange needed someone.

'Can you make shoes?' she asked. I lied and said yes, figuring I would learn on the job and I did! I did a bit of work there and they kept asking me back and I continued working mostly at the Royal Exchange. I was a dyer, milliner, jeweller, costume prop maker, and finally got a full-time job there ending up as deputy costume supervisor. I worked for the Exchange for more than ten years (over 100 shows). It was a creatively exciting period for the theatre and I had a really good time and made good friends.

When I started thinking it was time for a change, someone I knew from the Royal Exchange now working for Granada Studios offered me a job. I moved to Granada and worked on many TV dramas which led to work first on low-budget films and then larger feature films. It was on one of these films that I met my future husband.

Sophie and Tony

We wanted to buy a house together but it was hard to find one in Manchester with the right aspect. This house kept coming on and off the market and we kept trying to view it but we were never around to be able to do so. Finally we were both free and viewed it and fell in love at first sight.

We moved in ten years ago in 2004; we were made to feel extremely welcome from the first day. There is a village atmosphere here and it is very convenient and quiet. It is near the hospital, which is now important to us since Stephen (Sophie's father) is now living with us.

Stephen's Journey

My father was a steelmaker in Sheffield in the family firm. Both my parents were Quakers from Quaker families and we had a large group of relatives in Sheffield. My mother became interested in the work of Maria Montessori and started a Montessori school when I was 3 which was held in our house. It became so popular that we had to move to larger premises. I attended it until I was 10 and then went to Abbotsholme Boys Boarding School in Derbyshire. I was there for seven years. It was a very progressive school, founded in 1890. It was very outward looking and tried to develop the child's interests and abilities and not be too constricted by exam results, and it suited me. It is still running as a coeducational school. I left around 1936 after taking my school certificate. I had always been interested in theatre so from there I went to Sheffield Art School for a couple of years, concentrating on fashion.

I'd already started to study at Reimann's School in London (it was a famous school in Berlin which had been driven out by Nazism and re-established in London) when war broke out and I returned to Sheffield. I was a conscientious objector and my objection was upheld by a tribunal in Leeds. There were a sizeable number of Jewish refugees in Sheffield and I worked on a committee to help them until they were all absorbed into normal life here.

By the time the war was over, I was left high and dry, as the refugee committee was no longer needed. Someone put me in touch with the Old Vic Theatre School which was offering training for designers, producers and actors in London. I applied for that very late but someone dropped out and they offered the place to me. The training was held in the theatre of that name on Waterloo Road – it was great and I enjoyed that immensely. I was sufficiently successful at the technical side of the training that they offered me a position on the staff. I stayed there until the school was closed down.

George Devine, one of the three creators of the Old Vic Theatre School, had started 'The English Stage Company' in Sloane Square, which is now the Royal Court Theatre. I designed a small number of productions there, one of which moved to the West End and was the first London production of *The Crucible*. I worked each year at Stratford as a men's cutter in their Wardrobe Department. This was when Laurence Olivier and Vivien Leigh were there. I worked on *Twelfth Night, Macbeth* and *Titus Andronicus.*

On 23 May 1956, I married Wendy, one of my students from The Old Vic, in Nottingham. She was born in India but the family was based in Loughborough and Nottingham. In the early 1960s, I was invited by the newly built Nottingham Playhouse to set up a course on theatre design at the art school and, with an architect colleague of mine, designed a course that could link with the new playhouse. I ran this course until the artistic directors Michael Elliot, Casper Wrede and James Maxwell, all ex-students of the Old Vic School, who were setting up the Royal Exchange Theatre in Manchester, offered me the job of resident designer. I continued to work here until I retired.

I started having treatment at Manchester Eye Hospital for macular degeneration. However, my sight deteriorated violently and as a result I decided to give up my flat in Disley and I have been happily incorporated here with my daughter and son-in-law ever since. I am very happy to live in this community and I enjoy the company and friendship of my close neighbours.

RESIDENTS IN 1911	RESIDENTS IN 2014
BOULAGE, George Galbois Born: 1870 Manchester Lancashire Occupation: Grey Cloth Merchant	Tony Born: 1954 London Occupation: Boom Operator in the film industry
BOULAGE, Frances Galbois Born: 1871 Leeds Yorkshire Occupation: Wife	Sophie Born: 1962 London Occupation: Costume Supervisor (theatre, TV and film)
	Stephen Born: 1919 Sheffield Occupation: Retired Theatre Teacher and Set and Costume Designer

Farah and Abdul

───※◆※───

Farah and Abdul have lived on the street since 2002

Left to right: Safa, Irfaan, Farah, Abdul and Saba

Farah's Journey

I was born in Salford in 1967, the oldest of six children and the only sister to five brothers. My father made cables for Ward and Goldstone, a factory on Frederick Road in Salford. My mother was a housewife. My parents had an arranged marriage. She was from Burewala, south of Faisalabad, and came to Salford after she married my father, who was from Gogmal near Gojra but was already living in Salford. I went to Halton Bank Primary School (now flats!) and then to Buile Hill High School where I did CSEs and my 16+. After that I went to Pendleton College and studied business and then worked as a trainee in various offices.

In 1985, I went with my family to visit Pakistan partly to visit family and partly to look for partners for me and my brother. Abdul introduced himself to me as I was returning from the showers! He was a distant relative (our grandmothers were sisters). We liked each other and so, with our parents blessing, we decided to get engaged and I went back to England. In September 1989, I returned to Pakistan for my brother's wedding. We decided we might as well get married then, too. So it was a partially arranged marriage. After we married I went back to Salford for a year and then moved to Pakistan to live with my husband for another year. We came back together to Salford in June 1991.

Abdul's Journey

I was born in a village called Saabchak in Faisalabad, Pakistan, in 1964. My father came to Faisalabad from Jalandhar in India (before the Partition) as a young boy. He was a farmer with only a couple of years of schooling. His father (my grandfather) was killed in India by four others; he walked home after the attack and collapsed when he got there. He was a very brave and strong man and a bit of a rebel. My mother, who was born in Pakistan, was a housewife with no schooling. I am their fourth child of nine (two sisters and six brothers). I went to school in my village and then to the local high school. Like my grandfather, I too was a bit of a rebel and I didn't do much for a year and a half after leaving school until my brother, who was working in the clothing business, left to work in a bank. I took over the shop in 1984 and worked there until 1991. When I left to go to England another of my brothers took over the shop.

Farah and Abdul

Abdul: We stayed in Salford for a year where I worked in the clothing trade as a factory machinist making jeans and then when I was promoted we moved to Bolton where I continued in clothing in a management role. We lived in Bolton for two years and then moved back to Salford where we stayed for twelve years. In Salford I started up a taxi business while continuing in the factory for some time. I had worked very hard and worked my way up. The factory owners appreciated my hard work and let me arrange my own schedule. But I liked taxi driving and was able to earn more so I left the factory and now I own a fleet of taxis and drive one myself.

Farah: By 1998 we had four children and we needed a bigger house and then later we also wanted to be closer to work and school (the girls were in Broad Oak Primary School in Parrswood and Abdul's work as a taxi driver was based in South Manchester). We had been looking for six years. Abdul knew the area from driving around. He found this house when he was helping a friend to buy a house and saw it in the Halifax. He asked about it and put in an offer while I was away in Pakistan. The house was a compromise because it was on a corner and didn't have a private garden, which was one of my main requirements, but the garden was nice, and it had plenty of rooms. There was a bidding war with sealed bids but we weren't going to let go of it and we won. We have never regretted it.

The house needed major modernisation as nothing had ever been done to it at all. It still had the old round plug sockets which were crumbling away and no central heating. It was owned by a violin maker, and all his wood was stored here at a certain temperature. We fixed it up (for nine months it was chaos) and have been in the house twelve years now. Originally, we didn't really like South Manchester and thought that the area would be too noisy but it is quiet despite being near to a main road and to Curry Mile. The children enjoy living here and have always been able to invite their friends round. We're glad we chose this house. When we met the neighbours we knew we had made the right choice. We have sometimes left doors unlocked by mistake, but nothing has ever been taken.

RESIDENTS IN 1911

TINDALL, Herbert Woods
Born: 1866
Margate Kent
Occupation: Merchant Oil

TINDALL, Sarah Ellen
Born: 1865
Manchester Lancashire
Occupation: Wife

LEWIS, Sarah
Born: 1884
Swansea Carmarthenshire
Occupation: General Servant
Domestic

RESIDENTS IN 2019

Farah
Born: 1967
Irlam O' the Heights, Salford
Occupation: Housewife

Abdul
Born: 1964
Faisalabad, Pakistan
Occupation: Taxi Driver

Irfaan
Born: 1994
Salford

Saba
Born 1996
Salford

Safa
Born: 1998
Salford

Mehraan
(Not pictured.)
Born: 1991
Salford

Claire and Andrew

Claire and Andrew have lived on the street since 1999

Left to right: Andrew, Jessie and Claire

Claire's Journey

I was born in 1968 in Ladysmith, South Africa. I have since found out that it is connected with Rusholme and Victoria Park because it was named after Lady Smith, the Spanish wife of Sir Harry Smith, who was a governor of the Cape Colony. At one point in his career Sir Harry and Lady Smith lived here in Victoria Park for several years. My family moved to Grahamstown (an 1820 settlers' town in the Eastern Cape) when I was 11. Dad was born in Kenya but was of British extraction and Mum was born in Bergville in Natal. He was a farmer and Mum was a primary school music teacher. I have a twin brother and one other brother. After high school I went to Rhodes University, also in Grahamstown, and studied social work. After graduating, like many other young South Africans, I had a year out and came to England in 1993. I stayed with an aunt in Taunton and applied for jobs. I thought I would get a job waitressing or something similar but within a few weeks of arrival one of the social work jobs I had applied for accepted me. It was in Wilmslow and I moved to Cheadle. I liked living in England very much and decided not to return to South Africa. I've lived in South Manchester ever since.

Andrew's Journey

I was born in Barston, Warwickshire, a small village just outside Solihull, in 1960. My father was a country vicar so we moved around a bit connected with his work. At 3, I moved to Openshaw in East Manchester, at 8 to South London and at 16 to Norwich (hence my support for Norwich City!). My mum was a teacher and went back to teaching when I was about 11 or 12. She had four children under the age of three and a half at one point. I have two older sisters and a twin sister. Both Claire and I are twins.

After I finished school I had a gap year, working and travelling, before Birmingham University. After graduation, I worked as a volunteer in a night shelter for homeless men in Liverpool, which was attached to Liverpool Cathedral (Paddy's Wigwam). Then after two years postgraduate training at Newcastle University I worked as a probation officer in Newcastle on Tyne. I later moved to Manchester and have worked in various local authorities in social services in Manchester and Cheshire. Claire and I met when we both worked in Warrington. I currently work in Bolton. Claire and I moved here in October 1999.

Claire and Andrew

Why this street? We were looking for somewhere to live and I (*Andrew*) recalled being at a party at another house on the street and liking the house and the location. So when I went cycling around looking at potential houses and came here I saw this house was for sale. We liked it as soon as we viewed it. We love living here. Sometimes we get fed up with city life (litter, crowds, cars chewing up the verges), but it's a great location. It is convenient for work for both of us: walking to the university (*Claire*) and getting to Bolton is easy (*Andrew*). There is a good mix of people on the street. We already knew some of them through church and we have made many more friends here.

It is good being at this end of the street as it is nice seeing people walking past. It is nice having the church nearby. We like listening to the music as it wafts through our garden during the services. If the chips are down there are neighbours who would look out for you. People are friendly. There is a concern on the street for each other. We like the multiculturalism, too.

Jessie

I was born here in 2005 and now I am in Year 3 at St James'. I like living here because there are plenty of kids to play with. It is not really a busy road. Lots of the kids on our street are at my school. I like being able to walk to school and to the parks, Birchfields and Platt Fields, which are great!

RESIDENTS IN 1911

BROUNSTON, William
Born: 1846
Exeter Devon
Occupation: Agent For
Woollen Manufacts

BROUNSTON, Mary Emily
Born: 1855
Manchester Lancashire
Wife

BROUNSTON, Lilian Margaret
Born: 1879
Manchester Lancashire
Daughter

BROUNSTON, Helen Roylance
Born: 1886
Manchester Lancashire
Daughter

NUTT, Ernest Edward
Born: 1880
Bristol Somersetshire
Occupation: Agent For
General Drapery

SCHLEE, Walter Otto
Born: 1887
Hamburg Germany
Visitor

RESIDENTS IN 2019

Andrew
Born: 1960
Barston, Warwickshire
(outside Solihull)
Occupation: Social Worker

Claire
Born: 1968
Ladysmith, South Africa
Occupation: Lecturer in Social
Work, University of Manchester

Jessie
Born: 2005
Manchester
Daughter
Occupation: School pupil

Graham and Sabine

Graham and Sabine have lived on the street since 2009

Left to right: Zara, Graham, Sabine and Clarissa

Graham's Journey

I was born in Oxford in 1954. I have one brother. My dad grew up in Birmingham and my mum was from Norfolk, both of them coming from large families. They met at the end of the war in a demobilisation camp (my mum was in the land army and my dad had been a prisoner-of-war in Germany for four years, where he survived by working in his trade as a baker). After they married they came to Oxford for work, and at one point my dad worked for the Cadena Bakery. My mum was a full-time homemaker and volunteer worker in her church. I grew up in Oxford and went to primary school there and then to Oxford School. I was a keen boy scout in my youth and my interest in study came later! In 1972, I went to Portsmouth Teacher Training College and trained to be a religious education teacher in secondary schools. My parents were churchgoers and had a real faith and our whole family went to church. From my teenage years I had a personal faith and was very involved in a Christian youth club as well as with scouting.

I graduated as a teacher in 1976, got married and then taught for four years in Havant (near Portsmouth). In 1980, I started working with students as a staff worker for a Christian organisation in London and Kent, which necessitated moving. By 1985 I had three children: Simon (1980), Alice (1981) and Joy (born in 1985). In that year my wife and I felt the call to be missionaries and went to Missionary Training College in Hertfordshire, returning afterwards to teach in a secondary school in Kent for another year before going to the Philippines as missionaries. While we were in the Philippines my wife sadly died, and I returned to Gravesend with the children in 1987. I then became a church community worker and worked amongst the local ethnic community, mostly with South Asians. I met Sabine in 1988 and we married in August 1989.

Sabine's Journey

I was born in 1959 in Lübeck, Germany. My dad was born in 1936 in Berlin and my mum in 1940 in Konigsberg, East Prussia (now a Russian enclave with a capital called Kaliningrad). When the British bombed Berlin my father and his mother went to his grandfather's home (thought to be a safe place) which was also in East Prussia. When the Russians came in 1945, however, eight million people fled towards the West and both my parents as small children and their families ended up near Lübeck. It was strange that both my parents, aged 9 and 5 at the time, were on the same ship as they fled west. And as it turned out, it was the last voyage that ship made, as it was blown up on its return trip. My parents actually met at a dance at a youth group in 1956 and married in 1959, after which I was born. I had a younger brother but he died in infancy. They developed the wanderlust and emigrated to South Africa in 1965, living first in Johannesburg, then in Cape Town and finally in Durban. My father worked for Siemens, rising to become their Director of Telecommunications. I went first to a German school and then an English convent school in Durban. During my childhood we ran boarding and training kennels on our farm and my parents entered our seven German shepherds in shows – dogs were our family's life!

We returned to Germany for several reasons in 1973 when I was 14 – my grandmother was a widow by then, my parents wanted me to complete my education in Germany, and also because of the political situation in South Africa. I finished my A-levels equivalent in 1977. That summer I went with a youth group from church to a Christian community in France and had a life-changing experience. I decided to give my life to Jesus and became a Christian. On my return to Germany I studied *SozialPaedagogik* (science of teaching and social work), graduated in 1980, and then did a training year in Lübeck, working in a centre for mentally and physically handicapped young people. I stayed in Huemoz near Lausanne, Switzerland, in a Christian community and Bible college the following year, partly studying theology and partly working in the community. In 1983, I came to England and trained at London Bible College for two years before working in the East End of London in a church centre of the Shaftsbury Society. I went to a conference at Launde Abbey in Leicestershire in November 1988, where I met Graham.

Graham and Sabine

We got married in August 1989 and then worked together for fifteen years for a Christian organisation in the south of England, doing church community work, during which time we also studied more theology and had two more children. Zara was born 1991 and Clarissa in 1996, to join our older children, Simon, Alice and Joy. In 2004, we went to Berlin with Zara and Clarissa, helping local churches reach out to ethnic communities. It was lovely for Sabine to go back as an adult and for the children to see some of their mother's background.

After four years there we wanted to come back to the UK to work with students. There was an opening in Manchester, so we moved here in July 2008. Initially we rented a house in Northenden and attended Holy Trinity Platt Church here in Rusholme even though we were not living in the area. We were thinking we would like to be living nearer to the church and to the university when a 'God-incidence' (not a co-incidence, in our minds) occurred. The then owners of this house returned from Hong Kong for a holiday and were looking to sell it. They attended Holy Trinity and told the vicar. We had just asked him whether he knew of any suitable houses a few days before and after the owners spoke to him he mentioned it to us, and the rest was history. We moved here in February 2009, renting until we sold our house in Kent and then we bought our lovely home. Zara went to Xaverian and Clarissa went to Trinity High School - Clarissa is now at Xaverian.

We were warned against living in Rusholme but ignored the warnings because we liked the house and location. It was similar in size and style to our house in Kent. Now that we are here we like the street, and that it is so international. We are very happy there is a residents' association that is caring about the community, but disappointed that our working hours mean we can't often get involved. It is quiet, especially considering that we're so near the busiest bus route in Europe. We love the alleyway behind the houses with all the trees and blackberries! The location is good for schools and very handy for our work and family. Both the girls' friends and our student friends can visit easily. Marley, our labrador/springer spaniel, loves it here too!

RESIDENTS IN 1911	RESIDENTS IN 2019
GARDNER, Samuel Born: 1875 Broughton Lancashire Occupation: Estate Agent	Graham Born: 1954 Oxford Occupation: Christian Charity Staff Worker
GARDNER, Ellen Born: 1881 Greenheys Manchester Lancashire Wife	Sabine Born: 1959 Lübeck, Germany Occupation: Christian Charity Staff Worker
GARDNER, Leonard Born: 1908 Moss Side Manchester Lancashire Son	Zara Born: 1991 Gravesend, Kent Daughter Occupation: Volunteer at Birch Community Centre
VALLANCE, Jane Born: 1847 Ruthin North Wales Mother In Law	
VALLANCE, Elizabeth Emma Born: 1882 Greenheys Manchester Lancashire Occupation: Drapers Assistant	Clarissa Born: 1996 Gravesend, Kent Daughter Occupation: Student

Elaine and Max

Elaine has lived on the street since 1979

Elaine and Max

Elaine's Journey

My father's parents were originally from Lithuanian Poland. His parents emigrated to America as young children in the mid 1880s. They married in about 1904 and set up housekeeping in South Bend, Indiana, where my father was born in 1905. After graduating in electrical engineering from Purdue University he worked in various jobs including designing airport runway lighting but spent most of his working life at Indianapolis Power and Light Company, selling electric heating.

My grandparents on my mother's side came from the Vilnius area; my grandfather, escaping from being drafted into the Czar's army, arrived in New York with five roubles in his pocket. He first moved to Cincinnati where my mother was born and then on to Indianapolis. He and my grandmother ran a small sweet shop at one point and in later life he worked in a factory making caps.

My parents met in Indianapolis through friends. My father lived in a boarding house with a friend who was going out with someone who was best friends with my mother. She left school when she was 16 and worked as a legal secretary and bookkeeper. Her boss wanted to send her to night school to be a lawyer, but she didn't take him up. She left work when my younger brother and I were born, but went back to the same company when I was 10; by now it was a building and construction company

I attended high school in Indianapolis, and then studied English language and literature at the University of Chicago. After graduating, I went to Stanford University in California, where I received an MA in Education and qualified as an English teacher, although I had never really planned to be a teacher. I started teaching in California, in 1965. In the summer of 1966 I went to Europe with a friend using money I had saved up from my first year of teaching, visiting Greece and Italy as well as all of the countries in the British Isles. On the ferry back from the continent there was a group of British students who had been singing in Europe and we shared a compartment on the train from Dover to London with one of them, who said she had a friend who was going to Stanford. I gave her my contact details, thinking that maybe I could be of help.

Having heard nothing on my return, I forgot all about it. But the following Easter I answered a call out of the blue from a PhD physics student from England who had been given my number. I invited him for tea. He brought some pictures from a jeep trip he'd made to Turkey and I had photos from my trip to Europe. It was the summer of love and we were in San Francisco. He said he was going to travel in South America after term finished, and did I want to come with him. I did, as I had really enjoyed my travels in Europe and was keen to do more. We travelled all the way from Mexico to Lake Titicaca in Bolivia, overland, mostly by bus, and flew back to San Francisco for the beginning of the next academic year. We married in 1968 and rented a bungalow in Palo Alto. When he finished his PhD in 1972 we came to the University of Manchester and lived in a flat in Didsbury before moving into 'Carolside' on Upper Park Road. We really liked Victoria Park but couldn't find a house here. Instead, we bought one in Withington. I worked at the University and also Manchester Polytechnic as it then was called, in various research and secretarial jobs – ending up as a research assistant in the Librarianship Department at the Poly.

In 1978, when I was seven months pregnant, we moved back to California, to Berkeley, for a job at the University of California and our first son was born. We returned to Manchester in July 1979 for a permanent job. We looked for a house in Didsbury, but they were all too expensive and so we asked the estate agent about houses in Rusholme and found this one. It was perfect and we already knew we liked the area. We moved in that autumn. The health visitor suggested I sign the baby up for St James' Primary School and join the 'Meet-a-Mum' group at the Birch Community Centre. I met mums from all over the world there, joined a baby-sitting circle and never looked back. I had a great circle of friends within a week; many are still friends today.

Our second son was born at St Mary's Hospital in 1981. I helped out at the children's playgroup, where I became leader after a couple of years, and then worked in patient participation and health promotion at Rusholme Health Centre.

When the boys were 10 and 13, I discovered that Section 11 Education (supporting children who didn't speak English as their first language and others who might be affected by racism) didn't require a UK teaching qualification so I started teaching again, at Princess Primary School in Moss Side until it shut down, then at Chevassut in Hulme, which also shut down and finally at Our Lady's in Whalley Range until I retired in 2007. We all loved living here, and in 2001 we extended the house. Although my husband moved out in 2011, I still love it here with the cats Benjy and Ivy and all my friends. I am secretary of the residents' group and get huge satisfaction getting to know people and from working for our community with neighbours and friends from all over the world.

Max

I loved living here and had many good friends on the street who I've known all my life. We played football in the old St Vincent de Paul school playground, had adventures in the back alley, which wasn't so nice then, and played cricket alongside my friend Thomas's house, down the street.

I went to Birmingham University and came back in 2003 to work for British Cycling. I moved into a flat in Didsbury with a friend and later bought a house in Levenshulme. I met my partner in 2004 and we now have two children. We lived here in the house for a year in 2007/8 when Mum and Dad were in America. We later moved to the south-west where I have a role in schools promoting sustainable development. We're very happy there but I do miss things about this area. One thing I have yet to find elsewhere is the strong sense of community and Mancunian warmth and generosity of spirit. Dorset may be beautiful, clean and have fresher air and nicer weather but it doesn't have Mancs!

RESIDENTS IN 1911	RESIDENTS IN 2019
PARITH, Arthur George Born: 1875 Rowley Regis Staffordshire Occupation: Engineer	Elaine Born: 1942 Indiana, USA Occupation: Retired High School English and Primary Infants Teacher
PARITH, Frances Nary Born: 1880 London Wife	Max Born: 1981 Manchester Occupation: Sustainability Officer
PARITH, Freda Joyce Born: 1906 Manchester Daughter	(Also Benjy and Ivy the cats, not pictured)
PARITH, Edna Mary Born: 1911 Manchester Daughter	

New Apostolic Church

The church has been on the street since 1955

The Sunday Congregation outside the new church building after Divine Service.

The New Apostolic Church began in 1832 in London and Albury, Surrey, as the Catholic Apostolic Church and reformed as of 1863 in Germany and Holland and later established as the New Apostolic Church.

The Church Today

The New Apostolic Church is an international Christian church. The foundation of its teachings is the Holy Scripture. It developed from the Catholic Apostolic Church in 1863 and is led by apostles, just like the first Christian congregations.

The New Apostolic Church recognises three sacraments: Holy Baptism, Holy Sealing and Holy Communion. Baptism with water is the first and fundamental act of the triune God's grace upon a human being who believes in Christ. Through the act of Holy Sealing, the baptised believer is filled with the Holy Spirit. This occurs through prayer and laying-on of hands of an apostle. The body and blood of Christ are imparted in the sacrament of Holy Communion.

The return of Christ to take home His bride is a central component of New Apostolic doctrine. Other significant elements are missionary work and love for one's fellow human being.

The New Apostolic Church is politically neutral and independent. It is financed by the voluntary donations of its members.

The New Apostolic Church has been active in Manchester for over sixty years and based here since 1955. During that time it has had four rectors: Priest Kern, Priest Peterson, District Evangelist Leo Aspden (rector 1985–2009 and 2012 –15) and Evangelist David Abrahamse (2009–12 and 2015 to present day).

The Church's Journey

The church has its roots in the nineteenth century. Around 1830, individuals and groups in England and Scotland began praying for an *outpouring of the Holy Spirit*. In the spirit of the *evangelical awakening* movement of the time, they understood this as a revival of Christian life within the various denominations, which had grown rigid in their formal structures.

An 'apostolic' movement came into being, which later took on church structures after twelve apostles were called between 1832 and 1835 by individuals who possessed the gift of prophecy. The distinguishing feature of the church, which now bore the name 'Catholic Apostolic Church', was that it was led by apostles who dispensed the gift of the Holy Spirit to believers through the laying on of hands in order to prepare them for the return of Christ, which they expected imminently.

Differences arose in response to the question of whether to fill the vacancies in the circle of the apostles, whose number had diminished first to ten, and by 1863 to six. When attempts to fill the vacancies in the circle of the apostles failed, a subsequent fundamental difference of interpretation concerning the role of the apostle ministry in the preparation of the believers for the return of Christ led to the separation of the Hamburg congregation from the apostles of the Catholic Apostolic Church in 1863.

Starting from the congregation of Hamburg, a new group of apostles began its activity and by 1864 the Dutch branch of the 'apostolic mission' to the Christian world had already been founded, with a small congregation in Amsterdam. The Hamburg congregation emerged under various names depending on the occasion. To distinguish themselves from the first 'apostolic congregations' the new congregations established over the ensuing period soon began referring to themselves as 'new apostolic congregations' in official correspondence. By the turn of the twentieth century, the Church became known as the 'New Apostolic Congregation' and, as of approximately 1930, as the 'New Apostolic Church'.

Despite growing rapidly throughout the world, it was not until the 1940s when the church in Canada initiated a mission to the United Kingdom, joining forces with German and South African members who came here during the war, that the church returned to its original roots. Today there are nine million members throughout the world.

Members based in Manchester initially travelled to Buxton, but in 1951 the congregation began to meet in members' houses in June Street (Chorlton on Medlock), Stamford Street (Old Trafford) and a hall on Deansgate. In 1953, the decision was taken to buy a doctors' surgery in Rusholme and the ground floor was converted into a church. The first service was held two years later and the first minister, Priest Kern, and his family moved in upstairs.

Today there are 150 active members in Manchester and the wider northwest as far afield as Liverpool and even Abergele, with around eighty attending most Sundays. Members have seventeen countries of origin between them, including the UK, Zambia, Congo, South Africa, Germany, Switzerland, Austria and Ghana. There are about thirty children and an active youth group and a choir.

Renate and Leo

Leo and Renate

Leo's Journey

My mother, Irmgard, was brought up in Hanover, Germany, where she was a member of the congregation as a child. Her parents died when she was young and she moved in with her brother and his wife, losing contact with the church. She met my father Thomas, an Englishman, in Germany after the war and they settled in Darwen where I grew up, the youngest of five children.

When I was about 20, my mother developed the desire to go to church. My father took her to the local parish church, amongst others, but she did not feel at home. So she wrote to the New Apostolic Church in Hanover. Although she had no current address for the church, the letter found its way to a retired priest who remembered her confirmation. He sent it on to the District Evangelist in Birmingham who in turn contacted Priest Petersen who was rector in Manchester at the time. As a result, he visited my parents and invited them to attend services here. Mum walked into our humble church building, and announced: '*I am home*'.

My father used to drive her and, over time, became involved in the church and eventually became a deacon in 1981. Initially, I played football on Sundays, but realised that I would have the chance to use the car and practise driving if I acted as their chauffeur. I used to listen to the radio in the car and then would drive them back again after the service. After a few months, I decided to come into the services to see what they were about, got interested and found my faith. I was ordained a priest in 1984 and the same year Renate and I were married.

In October the year after our marriage (1985), Priest Petersen, who had been rector for twenty-one years, retired and – at just 25 years old – I was commissioned with the responsibility of taking his place. The same year I started work for Pilkington's (as my ordinary job) in north Manchester and moved to Whalley Range which made things much easier than travelling in from Darwen for me to carry out my ministry and my job. My parents moved into the flat above the church at the same time and, with great devotion, cared for the building and its grounds and for many members of the community for over a decade.

Renate's Journey

I grew up in Berlin and, following school, I first trained as a dental nurse, and then later worked for the social services. I enjoyed travelling with friends and on one of my trips (in 1983), I went to Scotland where the New Apostolic Church was holding a youth weekend. Leo was there and that's where we first met. Within a year we were married. When we later moved to Manchester we were closer to the church and I enjoyed visiting some of the elderly members of the congregation there. After raising our two boys I trained as a teacher at North Trafford College and Bolton University and later as a professional language trainer in German and English.

At church, I work with the children's groups and do Sunday School lessons for them during the services. I teach the 3-8 year olds alongside other members of the team who provide great support and teaching for the children up to confirmation at the age of 15.

Leo and Renate

At Easter 1998 the last divine services were held in the old building before it was taken down by hand and rebuilt using the recycled bricks. Services continued but were temporarily held at Hulme Hall, Manchester YMCA and the Campanile Hotel in Salford until, a year later, the new building had been completed and the congregation returned for Easter Sunday. The church was dedicated by the District Elder Duemke on 16 May 1999.

Our biggest wish is that the congregation can become a closer part of the community. The congregation is so geographically far spread and services are held twice a week (on Sunday mornings and Wednesday evenings), so it is not always easy, but we would really like to be open and neighbourly and reach out to the local community. We have been pleased to be able to host residents' meetings in the church and hope that we can find ways to participate mutually in events. We now actively support a local food bank around key events such as Harvest Thanksgiving and Christmas. It is our strong wish that we would very much like to be able to give something back.

RESIDENTS IN 1911	PASTOR IN 2015
The house on the site was not occupied in 1911	**Leo** Born: 1960 Darwen, Lancashire Occupation: District Evangelist and Rector (voluntary); Management Consultant and Executive Coach **Renate** Born: 1962 Berlin, Germany Occupation: Teacher (Sunday School) and Professional Language Trainer in German and English

Student House (1)

The group lived on the street from September 2015 to July 2016

Back row, left to right: Ben, Tanmayee (Tammy).
Front row, left to right: Helena B, Marie and Helena A.

Helena A's Journey

My father is from Barrow-in-Furness and my mum is from Hong Kong. My parents met while they were both working at a summer job in a pie factory when they were at university. I have a sister three years older than me. My dad was working as a lecturer at Wolverhampton University in human computer interaction when I was born but soon after my birth the family moved to Portsmouth where he worked at the University there. I grew up and went to school in Portsmouth until Sixth Form when I went to boarding school in Wimborne. My granny and my uncle live in Manchester, which is one of the reasons I wanted to come here. I liked Manchester and the university is good in the field. For most of my life I wanted to do medicine but by the beginning of the Sixth Form when I had to start making university applications I decided I didn't want to do it after all. I always liked biology – it was my favourite subject – and I liked the sound of neuroscience (next year, though, I am switching course to biomedical science). I came to Manchester in 2014 and lived in halls in Whitworth Park in my first year. A group of six of us were looking for a house together. It was hard to find a house big enough in our price range – all the others we saw were tiny, cramped and expensive! We found this through Manchester Student Homes and when we came to see it we said, 'Yes'!

Helena B's Journey

My mum is from Enfield and my dad from Ware, both in Hertfordshire. They met at a mutual friend's party. My mum worked for the Fire Service headquarters and my dad was doing contracting for engineering when I was born. We've always lived in Stone (7 miles from Stevenage). I was brought up there and went to the local primary in Stone and to secondary in Ware. I am an only child. When I started looking around for a university it was a spur-of-the-moment decision to look at Manchester – it was three days before their open day. I came and liked it and, after my interview I liked it some more! I liked biology and neuroscience seemed interesting. I was in Richmond Park Halls in Fallowfield my first year. I met most of the others through the course.

Setor's Journey

I was born the middle of three sisters in Accra where my father was a film producer. When I was 7 or 8 my mother moved to the UK to become a nurse, first in Bradford and then in London. We came as a family to visit her in Fulham and then, when I was 12, we moved to East Acton in London where my family still lives and where I went to school.

I went to Liverpool University to study audio production because I wanted to do the course and it was well away from home. When I got the grades, I was accepted at Manchester University to do a Masters in Audiology, moving on to the medical side of things. At first I commuted and then found this house. I really like it; there are nice people living here and it has a good atmosphere. The area is quiet and the neighbourhood is a nice place. I will shortly need to apply for jobs and hope to be able to stay in the north.

Helena and Helena: We like it here; everything is close by; there is lots of good food. It's surprisingly very nice here which is unexpected after seeing Curry Mile! Our friends from other universities are amazed at how nice the street is. We'll be moving on next year since Hazel will be going on her medical placement and we won't have enough people for the house.
Helena A: And I like being able to see my granny and uncle every Sunday, too.

RESIDENTS IN 1911	RESIDENTS IN 2015
BEATY, Lillie Born: 1876 Manchester Lancashire Occupation: Widow, Private Means	Helena B Born: 1995 Stevenage, Hertfordshire Occupation: Undergraduate, University of Manchester in Neuroscience
BEATY, Sheila Lilian Born: 1903 Denbeigh North Wales	Ben Born: 1995 Stockport Occupation: Undergraduate, University of Manchester in Neuroscience
BEATY, Erica Mary Born: 1905 Denbeigh North Wales	

BEATY, Dora Marguerite
Born: 1906
Denbeigh North Wales

GITTINS, Marguerite Lilian
Born: 1894
Horwick Lancashire
Occupation: Servant Domestic

Marie
Born: 1996
Sharoe Green, Preston
Occupation: Undergraduate,
University of Manchester in
Neuroscience

Tanmayee (Tammy)
Born: 1995
Pune, India
Occupation: Undergraduate,
University of Manchester in
Electrical Engineering

Helena A
Born: 1996
Wolverhampton
Occupation: Undergraduate,
University of Manchester in
Neuroscience

Hazel
(not pictured)
Born: 1996
Sharoe Green, Preston
Occupation: Studying Medi-
cine, University of Manchester

Setor
(not pictured)
Born: 1995, Accra, Ghana
Occupation: Postgraduate
Master's in Audiology,
University of Manchester

Afzal and Rowshanara

The family has lived on the street since 1992

Left to right: Afzal, Mumeenul and Rowshanara

Rowshanara's Journey

I grew up in Bangladesh and went to school there. I moved to England in 1977, to join my husband who was already here, in the Stockport area. My husband probably chose to come to Stockport because there were some people here related to us but I don't really know why he chose Stockport. By the time I came here there were a few people we knew but mostly I lived happily at home. I didn't have to do anything because he took care of it all before I got here. We lived in different places but we wanted a big house so my husband found this house by looking at an estate agent.

I like living here. Everybody is nice.

Afzal's Journey

My parents were born in Sylhet in Bangladesh. My dad was a teacher there. He came over to Stockport in the Sixties on his own, looking for better opportunities, and ran a business there – a restaurant located near the town centre. My mother came later, after they married. After living in Stockport we moved to Longsight and then Levenshulme before our family came here in 1992, as we needed a bigger house by then and we liked the area. Before attending Burnage High School, I went to Alma Park Primary School in Levenshulme and prior to that, to St John's in Longsight. After college I went to work. I have had various jobs, in banks, insurance, research and with the RAC, all in the financial sector, and now I am an insurance broker. I married in 2004 in Bangladesh and my wife came to Manchester to join me in 2005. Mumeenul was born in 2006 and he is now a pupil at St James'. We like living here. It is quite central and there are many different communities all getting on together. It is getting to be a famous street, with all the parties every year!

Mumeenul

I like it here. There are lots of sweet shops. I like my school and I have lots of friends.

RESIDENTS IN 1911

ALMOND, Charles F
Born: 1880
Manchester
Occupation: Paper Merchant

ALMOND, Ethel C
Born: 1883
Oldham
Wife

ALMOND, Frederick W
Born: 1908
Manchester
Son

ALLCOCK, Alethea E
Born: 1892
Waingrove Derbyshire
Occupation: Servant

RESIDENTS IN 2019

Afzal
Born: 1977
Stockport
Occupation: Insurance Broker

Rowshanara
Born: 1952
Sylhet, Bangladesh
Occupation: Retired;
Mother/Grandmother

Mumeenul
Born: 2006
Manchester
Occupation: Pupil at St. James
C.E. Primary School

Bilkis (not pictured)
Born: 1982 Manchester
Occupation: Customer
Services Advisor, Bank

Jasmin (not pictured)
Born: 1983, Sylhet, Bangladesh
Occupation: Housewife

Mueedul (not pictured)
Born: 1992, Manchester
Occupation: Accounts
Assistant

Arefa (not pictured)
Born: 1999, Manchester
Occupation: Student,
Manchester Academy

(just after Lockerbie) and then later that year I started at Trafford General and became a community midwife covering Old Trafford and Stretford, a role I've carried out ever since. Trafford General closed four years ago and has been taken over by Manchester Central Health Authority so I am based at St Mary's now. But I am still a community midwife and I am still working in Stretford/Old Trafford.

Sean and Ellen

My (*Sean's*) cousin married Ellen's sister in 1994. We met before her engagement do and at family gatherings after that. We married in 1995 and had some building work done on the house before moving in together six months later.

We like living in Manchester. The street is convenient for getting to town, to work, to the airport. We like it here and don't see anywhere better. It's changed a bit, with a bigger Asian community and a bigger mix. It's gone up in the world. There's nowhere better!

Kate

I was born in 1996 at Trafford General Hospital. I went to St Kentigern's Primary School and then to Loreto High School in Chorlton. Now I am at Xaverian College in my first year. I'm studying maths, biology, chemistry and Spanish. I like animals and am hoping to be a vet. I have done placements on dairy farms, at veterinary surgeries, battery hen farms and riding stables.

Laura

I was born in 1998 and also went to St Kentigern's and Loreto. I am now in year 10 and about to start my GCSEs. I like walking in the countryside.

RESIDENTS IN 1911	RESIDENTS IN 2019
KING, Alice Born: 1864 London Occupation: Boarding House Keeper	**Sean** Born: 1955 Boyle, County Roscommon, Republic of Ireland Occupation: Construction and Civil Engineering
TAYLOR, Eveline Nybertall Born: 1889 Plymouth Lodger, No Occupation	**Ellen** Born: 1957 Longsight, Manchester Occupation: Community Midwife
HUGHES, Sydney Born: 1895 Pystill, Carnavonshire Occupation: General Servant Domestic	**Kate** Born: 1996 Trafford General Hospital Rusholme, Manchester Occupation: College Student
	Laura Born: 1998 Rusholme, Manchester Occupation: High School Student

Dezi and Abigail

Dezi has lived on the street since 1975; Abigail since 2011

Dezi and Abigail

Dezi's Journey

My parents both came from Ireland – my father, Frank, from Fintona, County Tyrone, and my mother, Kathleen, from Ballyhale, County Kilkenny. They came to England looking for work, met each other in Manchester in a pub called 'The Robin' on Hyde Road and married in Holy Name Church on Oxford Road on 2 January 1954. My dad was a crane driver and he died in June 1976, one of the hottest summers on record, so he was not here in this house very long. My mum had several jobs. At one time she worked in a hospital. She also used to keep lodgers and would go to Victoria Train Station with a priest and a bus to meet the young Irishmen who had just come in from Holyhead. She told them to 'get on the bus' if they wanted a job and a clean place to stay. She had sixteen houses at one time.

There were seven of us (Eileen, who lives two doors down from me now, Frances, who used to live on the street, too, Kathleen, Margaret, Mike, Bernadette and me). I was the youngest. We lived a few streets away when I was born, but the house had become not quite big enough for all of us. When she saw this house my mum fell in love with it so we moved here. She paid £7,000 for it.

We all went to St Edward's Primary School, which originally was located behind the church on Thurloe Street in what is now the parish hall, and Margaret and I went to St Pius, which turned into St Vincent de Paul High School.

My earliest memories are being in the garden at our first house and then in the garden here. Mum grew tomatoes there. After my dad died, Eileen got married and moved on the street, then, in 1978, Frances moved into another house on the street. Mum had a restaurant on Wilmslow Road called 'Farmhouse Kitchen'. She threw herself into the business. I used to go down with her in the mornings to set up for the day. We left here around 4.20 a.m. and in the winter the locks were frozen on the doors of the café. I went to school from there.

I learned to play the fiddle at the old St Edward's School, around the age of 6 (my dad was a fiddle player as well). They took me to dancing lessons but I didn't like that and then to learn the tin whistle but I cried. By the time I was in high school I was in a band and playing all over Britain. The van for the band would pick me up after school on Friday and drop me back early Monday morning in time for classes, and when I left St Pius I went straight into playing in bands both around Britain and internationally. I was in 'Toss the Feathers' – which was very successful at the time. There were lots of musicians in the area then. I am still playing and performing professionally. I have lived in this house ever since we moved here in 1975. My mum died on 2 May 2010.

I met Abi in Freemantle, Western Australia, in February 2010. I was touring and Abi was living there. One of the band members knew us both and introduced us on South Beach. The next day I flew home.

Abi's Journey

Although I was born in Kilkenny, I grew up in Tipperary. Mum and Dad owned a factory that sold glasses to wholesalers and bars, and were horse trainers as well. I was the youngest of four. I went to school in Ireland and in the year before A-levels (1996) I joined 'Riverdance' and travelled the world with them. I danced in Manchester in 1997 and in 2003 at the MEN arena. It opened a lot of doors for me. I was with them for four years full-time and on and off doing gigs here and there for another five years. I hadn't finished my education and it was expected that I would. I studied on tour and did my leaving certificate and then, having been inspired to be a physiotherapist by one of the physios on tour, I came to Manchester to do physiotherapy at the University of Manchester from 2000 to 2003. I lived in Longsight.

I moved to London after that and did four years of rotations there at teaching hospitals. I went to Australia to do a twelve-week module for my Master's degree in 2007. I fell in love with Australia and always planned to come back. I worked in Dublin for some months and then got a visa and went back to live in Perth from 2008 to 2010 but decided to leave in June 2010. I met Dezi on the beach in early 2010. When I flew home on Air Asia, Dezi picked me up at the airport. I tried to work in Ireland, but the recession made that difficult so I came here to do locum work and I have been living here since September 2011.

Dezi and Abi

Dezi: This house has been my home all my life. I bought my first fiddle off Eric Voigt (the violin maker who used to live nearby). It is very convenient here for work, too, and I can easily reach any part of the world as it's close to the airport. I really like it around here.

Abi: I knew Manchester as a student. It has taken me a while to get used to the weather here after Australia, but I do like the changing seasons. I do locum work at the hospitals. I met Halimo (who lives across the street) there when she was assisting in translations.

RESIDENTS IN 1911	RESIDENTS IN 2019
UTTLEY, Ethel, Mary Born: 1879 Hebden Bridge, Yorkshire Wife	**Dezi** Born: 1973 St Mary's Hospital, Manchester Occupation: Professional Musician **Abi** Born: 1978 Kilkenny, Ireland Occupation: Physiotherapist

Student House (2)

Holly came to the street in 2012 with her housemates moving in a year later

Left to right: William, Holly, George, Rory and Ovi

Ovi's Journey

I was born in Galați, Romania, in 1993. My mother is an economist for a veterinary equipment and pharmaceuticals firm and my father is a sales manager for an agricultural business. I went to Vasile Alecsandri National College in Galați, one of the top high schools in the country, where I studied foreign languages (including English for five hours a week), maths, and IT. I specialised in maths and physics.

I came to Britain because I always wanted to experience other countries and a life of my own. I came to Manchester because I didn't get into Glasgow University (my first choice). I am now happy about this because when I later went to visit Glasgow I didn't like it. Manchester is much better!

During my first year I lived in Wright Robinson Hall near Piccadilly Station but I didn't like living there because I found living in a hall very impersonal. So a friend and I started looking for a house for the second year. My friend George said his mate had a nice house so I came here for a house, not for any other reason. Besides studying, I have started a business, which I see as important for my self-development.

Holly's Journey

I was born in Leeds in 1992 and moved to Birmingham when I was 2 and then to Huddersfield when I was 12 (following my dad's work) where I did my GCSEs and A-Levels. My mother looks after the family and my dad is a consultant psychiatrist.

I came to Manchester because it is the best centre in Europe for life sciences research. I am intending to continue at Manchester to do a Master's next year after I complete my BSc.

I lived at Owen's Park my first year and I found this house by looking for student housing on the internet. I checked out another house besides this one but went for this one because I really liked it and the landlord, Richard. I moved here with four others, three of whom I knew from my college, in September 2012. They all left last summer and I got the others who now live here through a mutual friend, George.

Holly and Ovi

Both the house and the street are nice and we have a good landlord. The rent is slightly more expensive than elsewhere, but the water is included so it works out much the same. The house is big, with a shared living room and no mice, although there are slugs in the kitchen! We weren't expecting that. And an alarm goes off all the time a few doors away, which has taken some getting used to.

We don't like the walk to and from the Curry Mile at night. It is dodgy and we've seen drug dealers around. Despite feeling unsafe between here and the Mile, we do the walk because we have to.

We work very hard and that takes up most of our time so we are not really looking for a connection with the neighbourhood. Although it is nice to know there is a residents' association, we haven't gotten involved because we're only here a short time and don't feel we have much to offer. We have great nights as a household when we gather and play computer games, the five of us together!

RESIDENTS IN 1911	RESIDENTS IN 2014
JOHNSTON, Alexander Born: 1870 Kirkmore Wigtownshire Occupation: Draper Credit	**William** Born: 1993 Dewsbury, Yorkshire Occupation: Undergraduate in Physics with Astrophysics, University of Manchester
JOHNSTON, Jean Aitken Born: 1881 Glasgow Wife	**Holly** Born: 1992 Leeds Occupation: Undergraduate in Cell Biology, University of Manchester
JOHNSTON, Elizabeth Dryden Born: 1910 Manchester Daughter	**George** Born: 1992 Southampton Occupation: Undergraduate in Economics and Finance, University of Manchester
WOOLLEY, Gertrude Mary Born: 1893 Derbyshire Occupation: Domestic Servant	

Rory
Born: 1993
Hope Hospital, Manchester
Occupation: Undergraduate
in Electronic Engineering,
University of Manchester

Ovi
Born: 1993
Galați, Romania
Occupation: Undergraduate
in Mechatronic Engineering,
University of Manchester

Anthony and Eileen

Anthony and Eileen have lived in this house since 1977

Left to right: Kevin, Anne Marie and Eileen

Anthony's Journey

My father, Kevin, worked as a labourer both in England and with Bord Na Móna in Ireland. My mother looked after the family. There were ten children: two girls and eight boys. I was the fifth. I went to school in Longford until I was about 12 years old and started work first in Hart's Restaurant and then in the Longford Arms Hotel as a porter. At age 15, I came to Manchester with my brother Seamus. We stayed at first with our older brother and sister who were living in Longsight and I got a job. My parents and the rest of the family came soon afterwards and they got a house for us on Blackthorn Street in Beswick near Grey Mare Lane Market. The first time I ever saw a black person was on the train to Manchester. One of my first jobs was with Kilroe Civil Engineering when the firm was still young (they only had one van then) but I moved around from one firm to another doing similar work. I was a 'banksman'. (*NB. A banksman is the person who directs the operation of a crane from the point where loads are attached and detached.*) I have worked all over Britain and including Germany and the Isle of Wight since then.

I met Eileen at St Kentigern's one Sunday lunchtime in December 1975. There was an Irish musician, Seamus Shannon, playing there. The men in my family were from a long tradition of Irish musicians. My father played the banjo and Eileen's father was a violin player and the boys in her family were all musical. So you could say that we met through an interest in music.

Eileen's Journey

I was born on Summer Street in Chorlton-on-Medlock. My father was a wagon driver from Northern Ireland and my mother was from Southern Ireland. She kept lodgers once she was married but she had more than one job and at one time was manager of the Devonshire pub on Stockport Road. I was the oldest of seven children (five girls and two boys). We moved to Rusholme from Chorlton-on-Medlock and moved again. We came, finally, in 1974, to another house on this street when I was about 19. I attended St Edward's RC Primary School and then The Hollies. From there I did nursing at Withington Hospital. I qualified in June 1976 and met Anthony just before qualifying. We got engaged a week after meeting and married twenty-one months after that. I worked at Withington Hospital until it closed, and now I am a nurse practitioner at Wythenshawe Hospital.

Eileen and Anthony

We bought this house two weeks before we got married. We had tried for other houses on the street but weren't able to buy them as at that time it was hard to get a mortgage. This one was sold by Oystons. We put in an offer and they accepted it and took the house off the market. When we moved in we started repainting the walls, but by winter they were soaking wet. We hired someone to see what was wrong and when he looked in the loft he saw that the roof was full of holes. We have been fixing up the house ever since! We had five children here: Katie in December 1978, Anthony (TC) in 1979, Kevin in January 1986, Martin in September 1987, and Anne Marie in October 1989. All the kids went to St Edwards and then St Albans, which merged with St Vincent de Paul.

We love living here. It's handy for anything. We have very good neighbours on both sides and Ralf and Lida across the street. You don't have to drive anywhere. We're close to the hospital. It's very quiet and has always been a quiet street. Mum, before she died, lived two doors down and my sister Fran used to live on the street, too. My brother Dezi now lives in my mum's house.

Anne Marie

I love living here. It was great growing up here, playing out and playing in the old playground attached to the school. I remember when it snowed the whole space was untouched and beautiful. I still have lots of friends around here.

RESIDENTS IN 1911

WALLACE, Arthur Stanley
Born: 1886
London Middlesex
Occupation: Journalist

WALLACE, Gracie Purdee
Born: 1886
Rangoon Burma
Wife

WALKER, Elsie
Born: 1895
Manchester Lancashire
Occupation: Domestic Servant

RESIDENTS IN 2019

Anthony
(not pictured)
Born: 1954
Longford, Ireland
Occupation: Underground
Plant Operator

Eileen
Born: 1954
Chorlton-on-Medlock,
Manchester
Occupation: Registered
Studying Nursing

Kevin
Born: 1986
Manchester
Occupation: Unemployed

Anne Marie
Born: 1989
Manchester
Occupation: Studying Nursing
at University of Salford

Wal and Jill

Jill and Wal have lived on the street since 1986

Left to right: Manmohan (Moni), Gurpurshad (Jill) and Walaiti (Wal)

Wal's Journey

My granddad initially came to the UK from India in the 1940s or 50s to earn money and then returned to India with his earnings. He had three sons. My dad was the middle son. He came here with my granddad but, unlike my granddad, didn't go back. Instead, my dad brought my mum and me over when I was about 2 years old. We stayed for about a year in Hulme and then went back to India again, leaving my father here. Two or three years later we all sailed back to the UK (now including a sister) and settled in Hulme again – on Bonsall Street. That was about 1962. It was the old Hulme where people never shut their front doors. My dad was a licensed door-to-door salesman selling mainly clothes. He worked in a variety of places besides Manchester, including Coventry and Leicestershire.

After we were in England my parents had two more daughters. I went to school in Hulme. It was a very strange experience because I didn't know a word of English. From Hulme we moved to Lloyd Street. Then I went to Greenheys School on Great Western Street. Afterwards I went to Ducie High and did well there. I had a fantastic time. I finished Sixth Form in 1974 with decent grades and got my first break into the motor industry, getting full-time employment with an apprenticeship in motor vehicles with Knibbs, a Fiat car dealership on Pin Mill Brow. I fell into that by accident. Two years into the apprenticeship I married Jill. It was an arranged marriage as is the custom in our culture and had been arranged since Jill was 11.

Jill's Journey

My granddad came to England from Delhi with my grandma before the Second World War. After the war started, my grandma didn't like it here so they went back for a while and then returned later with my dad. They lived in Sutton Coldfield, London, and finally settled in Cardiff. They had a shop selling West Indian things. My dad went back to India to marry my mum who was from Jaipur in Rajasthan. They both came to Cardiff in 1955. I was born five years later. I went to Ninian Park Primary school and then Fitzalan High School. I left school and got married in Cardiff at aged 16 and moved to Manchester in 1976.

Wal and Jill

Jill: We lived with Wal's parents, stayed for two years and had our first child, a daughter, there, and then moved to Moss Side off Claremont Road in a tiny two-up-two-down house on Wheeldon Street. The street is no longer there. We lived on Wheeldon Street for five years and had another child. Then we got an opportunity to buy a house opposite Wal's parents.

Wal: We bought the house, which was probably not a good idea as it was too close. We were quietly thinking we should move and then stumbled onto this house. It was a lot to do with fate. The owner of this house (and he had several other houses too) lived near my mum; someone introduced us to him. The house had lodgers in it and was derelict. We went to see him and finally he agreed to sell it to us. People advised us against it but we bought it (despite the lodgers) on a mortgage in 1981, even though we were still paying on the one across the street from my mum. That was a lot of stress for us so we sold it and, after getting rid of the lodgers, one of whom we had to buy out, we moved in here.

Both: We lived in the house while it was being done up. There were holes in the ceiling and sinks in each room, but it had many original features, including the servants' bells. It was quite stressful living here through the alterations. The street itself was beautiful though, from a picturesque point of view. There weren't so many cars then. We had four children, none of whom were born while we were living here, but Moni celebrated his first birthday in this house, having moved in when he was 11 months old. The children went to Heald Place School and then to St Vincent de Paul High School although Moni had to go to St Peter's.

Wal: At that time I was still working for Knibbs. They had several offices and I had worked in Bolton as manager and then Sale where I was general manager for the group there. Knibbs was taken over and then the new company was taken over in turn. I was promoted and stayed on until I realised I could run my own business when I had an opportunity in 1993 to take on a Vauxhall franchise in Accrington. We didn't move to Accrington because my parents were here and the kids were settled in Rusholme, although I would have liked to. Our two sons joined the business after they left school. We've got used to commuting.

Both: This street was absolutely beautiful when we moved here. It was an oasis. We would see people in their gardens in the summertime and became friends. I got my neighbour Jerry Rogers a job as an accountant for Knibbs when I was in Sale. Nowadays people keep themselves more to themselves. One of our daughters lives in Birmingham but the others live locally and call themselves 'the exs'. We have five grandsons and one granddaughter. Four of the grandchildren were born here (their parents living with us at the time). Lately we have been feeling less secure here and thinking we might like a bigger kitchen, but we are quite settled and it is very convenient.

We bought the house next door accidentally. A brother and sister from Spain owned the house and were living there while studying. We got to chatting and they told us they were going back to Spain so we made them an offer. The house is very useful to us when we have family functions; in fact, it is a godsend.

RESIDENTS IN 1911	RESIDENTS IN 2019
(TWO HOUSES)	
GRANT, Frederick William Born: 1856 Deptford Kent Occupation: Civil Servant In Revenue	Manmohan (Moni) Born: 1986 Manchester Occupation: General Sales South Wales, Manager within the family business
GRANT, Annie Born: 1859 St Neots Huntingdonshire Wife	Gurpurshad (Jill) Born: 1960 Cardiff Occupation: Housewife
GRANT, Sidney Born: 1886 Manchester Lancashire Occupation: Sorting Clerk G P O	Walaiti (Wal) Born: 1957 Nabha, Punjab, India Occupation: Chairman of own business
GRANT, Frederick John Born: 1887 Manchester Lancashire Occupation: Cashier	

GRANT, Arthur Ernest
Born: 1888
Manchester Lancashire
Occupation: Warehouseman

GRANT, Vincent
Born: 1891
Seacombe Cheshire
Occupation: Clerk

BRYCE, David
Born: 1872
Belfast County Antrim
Occupation: Traveller Gas
Apparatus

BRYCE, Noil
Born: 1906
Birmingham Warwickshire
Son

BRYCE, Jessamy
Born: 1908
Manchester Lancashire
Daughter

YOOL, Janet
Born: 1880
St Andrews Fifeshire
Occupation: Servant

Annette and Tim

—⊰⊱—

*Annette has owned the house since 1998 and lived here until 2008,
and then, with Tim, from 2015*

Tim and Annette

Annette's Journey

My dad, a painter and decorator, was born in Southport and came to Derby to find work because his sister had married and relocated there. My mum (who was a medical secretary) was born in Derby. She was his second wife; his first had died from TB. He had fought in the war in the military police, and described himself and his comrades as 'battle fodder'. I was brought up in a terrace, in a typical working-class family. I have two half-brothers, one half-sister and one 'whole' brother. He designs aircraft engines in Derby.

I attended Noel-Baker School (named after the Socialist MP Nobel Peace Prize winner) and my parents wanted me to get a job after that, so I worked for three years in the local Unemployment Benefit Office, long enough to qualify for an independent grant to go to college. I did a youth and community qualification at Alsager College which was later absorbed into MMU and I really found my vocation working with young people. Since then I have also qualified as a social worker and worked with young people in the justice system, child protection and mental health.

I moved around the country for interesting jobs, and lived in Dortmund, Germany, after college and then in Buckinghamshire, Birmingham, Portsmouth, Southampton, finally coming to Manchester in 1997 to teach on the Salford University social work, and later community development, course. I was so pleased to come back north. I still remember how kind a bus driver was when I first arrived; nothing like Southampton. At first I lived with good friends (the only people I knew in Manchester – I had met them in Southampton) in a room in Longsight for six months. Whilst living with them I rode around on my bike looking for a house to buy because now that I had a permanent job I could get a mortgage. I rode around purposely looking on all the side streets off the main roads – I found a lovely street nearby but couldn't afford it – and noticed this beautiful house for sale. I bought it in 1998 and lived here until 2008, always with very interesting lodgers. I then let it to friends and moved to a flat in Castlefield overlooking the canal basin and Manchester outdoor arena. I was made redundant in 2009 and Tim moved in to help with the mortgage.

Now I am working part-time at the University of Manchester; I have always had links with their Community and Youth Work course and taught mental health there. I am also involved with our local community radio station, All FM 96.9, where I have volunteered for some years as a radio producer, trainer and presenter. The project works with vulnerable people to build confidence and community. After redundancy, community radio helped me to regain confidence and I did a radio production degree, partly with Radio Regen and then the Manchester College.

Tim's Journey

My dad came from Australia as a teenager. He was a secondary school teacher specialising in teaching geography. My mum was from Manchester and didn't have a career but spent her time raising kids. I have two brothers, one older and one younger. I was brought up in Swinton and lived there until I was 18, in the house where I was born. I went to Sheffield Polytechnic for three years and studied geography and environmental studies; I sometimes think I came out not qualified to do anything at all! I had been working as a gardener for Salford Parks in the summers when I was at college, and they said I could stay on. I've been there ever since – for thirty-two years – learning on the job. I do grounds maintenance, horticulture, playground maintenance and other related work. After the Poly I lived in Chorlton until I moved into Castlefield with Annette in 2009.

Tim and Annette

I had met Tim in 1997 through a colleague in Portsmouth who introduced me to his brother who lived in Manchester. Tim socialised in the same group and at a party during the Eurovision Song Contest when Israel was competing for the first time, we found ourselves in the kitchen discussing Palestine (we were both supporters) and we were together from then on.

The tenants who were renting my house, friends of ours – in fact it was Mike who brought us together – decided to return to Ireland, so we decided to return here. We moved in on 29 March 2015 to be reunited with an attic full of stuff and to find dry rot in the downstairs floor! We love being back, though there is a shortage of good pubs to walk to since the Welcome closed. Now we have to go to Fallowfield or into town. It is so quiet here compared to living in Castlefield.

We love the diversity here in the community. There are people from all over the world. We wouldn't swap it for somewhere else, even without the pubs! It is so close to town and easy to cycle there – fifteen minutes or a £1 bus ride. We have great neighbours and we like the great staff at the social services building behind us, doing good work with families.

RESIDENTS IN 1911	RESIDENTS IN 2019
MIDDLEBROUGH, Richard Born: 1856 Salford Lancashire Occupation: Retired Butcher	Timothy Born: 1960 Swinton Occupation: Gardener for Salford City Council
MIDDLEBROUGH, William Born: 1865 Salford Lancashire Occupation: Retired Butcher	Annette Born: 1956 Derby Occupation: Lecturer at University of Manchester in community and youth work
MIDDLEBROUGH, Ellen Born: 1869 Salford Lancashire Occupation: Retired	
MIDDLEBROUGH, Clara Born: 1881 Salford Lancashire Occupation: Retired	

Luke and Paul

Luke and Paul have lived on the street since 1988

Luke and Paul

Paul's Journey

My mother was from Rochdale and worked for The Cooperative (CWS) for a while. She met my father, who was from London, when she was working as a hairdresser in Pocklington in Yorkshire. He was an agricultural representative for an oil company and travelled to various farms in the area. They married in 1940 just after the war started and eventually moved to Whalley Range. He was exempt from National Service because of his work and she stayed home and looked after the family. I was the youngest of three children.

I went to Chorlton Park Primary School until I was 10 or 11 and then to Baguely Hall. I finished when I was 16. I had various jobs after I left school: first I worked for Sparrow Hardwicke Wholesalers in textiles which was in Piccadilly (my old boss died at age 94 just before Christmas); then for D.C. Thompson, printing comics, on Chapel Street in Salford for twelve years. We used to call it the Comic Factory and I know them all, the *Beano, Dandy, Judy, Beezer, Topper*. In 1982, I went to MMU and stayed there until I retired. I met my wife, Joyce, who was from Eccles, at the Postgraduate Club in the Burlington Rooms at the university in about 1979. We married at the Registry Office on Jackson's Row in town in 1980. From the time I knew her and during our marriage Joyce worked with troubled girls at Burford in Whalley Range and then at Longsight Community Centre. From there she worked at Birch Community Centre, at Manchester Federation of Community Centres and, finally, at Church House.

We lived first in my house on Dorset Avenue in Rusholme but moved to Birchfields Road in 1982 where we had our two children: Rachel, born in 1982, and Luke, born in 1984. Although I had done a lot of work on the house on Birchfields Road and wasn't keen to move, we hadn't realised how busy a street Birchfields Road was (two people were killed on the road while we lived there) and as our children were getting old enough to want to go out and about we felt we should go somewhere safer. Joyce was friendly with Elizabeth who lived on this street so when the people who were living across the street from her decided to move out, Elizabeth told Joyce and we came to look at it. Joyce liked the house so we bought it.

Both Rachel and Luke went first to St James' Primary and then to Trinity High School. When Joyce died in 2008, Luke came back from Leeds, where he had been studying, to do his Master's degree here at MMU. He's now working at Sainsbury's while he is looking for something else. We've always been happy here. It is quiet and was convenient for work – just about walking distance. It changed a lot when the school behind us went. We used to have problems before the alley behind the houses on this side of the street was gated. I like it gated; it's more secure. The area has always had a country feel and there were lots of friends for the kids around the same age.

Luke

I loved it here when I was a kid. It was a good place to grow up and play. It was very friendly and close to the parks. I used to like riding my bike around the alleyway with my friends.

I was at Leeds University from 2003 to 2008 working on a degree in cultural studies and media and then working. I did my MA in Critical Theory (psychology, philosophy and linguistics) after that at MMU and started a PhD. One of my teachers on the course was Linnie Blake, who used to live on the street, too.

RESIDENTS IN 1911	RESIDENTS IN 2019
COLE, Stanley Born: 1878 Huddersfield Yorkshire Occupation: Merchant Silk And Cotton **COLE, Margaretha** Born: 1886 Neustettin Germany Wife	Paul Born: 1944 Whalley Range, Manchester Occupation: Retired House Foreman, John Dalton Building, Manchester Metropolitan University Luke Born: 1984 Manchester Occupation: Working at Sainsbury's

Anandi and Mehmood

Anandi and Mehmood have lived on the street since 1997

Left to right: Neelam, Anandi, Waris and Mehmood

Anandi's Journey

I was born in Bombay, the daughter of an English mother who was the librarian at Cathedral and John Connon School and an Indian father who was chief engineer for Firestone International. They met in London while my father was taking an MSc in Marine Engineering at Poplar Polytechnic and where my mother was librarian. They had a Quaker wedding at Hampstead Meeting House in 1960 and moved out to India shortly afterwards. I have an older sister and a twin brother. I went to Cathedral and John Connon School.

Mum wanted us to attend university in the UK. To get a grant you had to be resident here for three years beforehand so we moved to this country in 1977 when I was 12 to enable my older sister to fulfil the residence requirement. Dad stayed with Firestone in India. In 1979 he took a post in Ghana with Firestone International and only came to England in 1981 after the political coup in Ghana. We went to stay with my auntie in Roslyn, Scotland, for a year where I attended Penicuik High School. Then Mum got a job at Friends Meeting House in London and I did my O-levels at Queen Elizabeth's Girls' School in Barnet. My Sixth Form was spent at Leighton Park, a Quaker boarding school in Reading, where Firestone paid my fees, and then I went to York University to read English and history in 1983.

I came to Manchester in 1986 to do a Postgraduate Diploma in art gallery and museum studies, and in August 1987 I got a job as assistant exhibition organiser at the Cornerhouse. I lived in Withington and then Dad lent me the £3,000 deposit to enable me to buy a small terraced house near here. I met Mehmood in 1989 through anti-racist campaigns which we were both involved with. He had come back to Manchester to try to sell his house in Burnage so that he could take up a position with the *Frontier Post*, a newspaper in Pakistan. But the housing market had crashed, so he was stuck here!

Mehmood's Journey

We are a Kashmiri family living in what is now Pakistan. Both my father and grandfather served in the British army and my father transferred to the Pakistani army when it was established. I came to Bradford on my own in 1967 to live with my grandfather and great-uncle in a big house on Arnold Street. My extended family were all textile mill workers. I went to Laytock Junior and Tong Comprehensive Schools. Both were violent schools with frequent punch-ups. I left school at 15 and didn't go to university until much later, when I got an MA and then a PhD. I was homeless in Bradford for a while after my grandfather died, of an industrial disease I think, and I drifted in and out of work around the country for quite a while. I came to Manchester for one day for an interview, got the job and moved into Hulme Crescents. Later I bought a house in Burnage. I was a lecturer at Central Manchester College and then at Preston College. After meeting Anandi we lived in Burnage until we moved here in 1998. I am now teaching in Beirut.

Anandi and Mehmood

We lived in the house in Burnage and got married in 1992. The first two children were born there but we wanted more space so we decided to buy somewhere bigger. I knew the area and liked it. This house was rented but we asked the Korean students living here for the landlord's details and bought the house from Mr Kwon, who had lived here during the 1980s himself. Before him, a hairdresser had made substantial alterations including our massive front doors. Elizabeth, a few doors down, told us people had nicknamed it the Kremlin! We bought it because this one was cheaper than next door. Our second daughter, Amiya Naseem, died shortly after we moved in. Everyone in the street was really kind, even though they didn't know us well. I fondly remember Elizabeth, who had also lost a child and who was terminally ill, being very supportive. Later we planted some trees in Platt Fields Park in memory of Naseem.

Mishaal and Waris were born from this house and have grown up here, first attending St James' School and then, like Neelam, Stretford Grammar School. The joy of living on this street is the sense of community and the acceptance of diversity. And it's so easy to access everything – swimming clubs, Kung Fu classes, BMX in Platt Fields, Royal Northern College of Music; you name it, you can find it here.

RESIDENTS IN 1911	RESIDENTS IN 2019
KNOWLES, Alfred Born: 1850 Lancashire Manchester Occupation: Retired Fish Salesman, Widower	**Mehmood** Born: 1957 Jhelum, Pakistan Occupation: Assistant Professor in Creative Writing, American University of Beirut, Lebanon
COUNTER, Gertrude Born: 1875 Lancashire Manchester Occupation: Dress Maker, Daughter & Widow	**Anandi** Born: 1964 Bombay (Mumbai), India Occupation: Lecturer in Media and Cultural Studies, University of Central Lancashire, Preston
COUNTER, Montsi Born: 1900 Lancashire Manchester Grandson	**Neelam** Born: 1994 Manchester Occupation: Intern with Quod, London
COUNTER, Alick Born: 1902 Cheshire Cheadle Hulme Grandson	**Mishal** (not pictured) Born: 1999 Manchester Occupation: Student at Stretford Grammar School
	Waris Born: 2001 Manchester Occupation: Student at Stretford Grammar School
	(not pictured) Imli the cat'

Hilary and Stuart

Hilary and Stuart have lived on the street since 1993

Stuart and Hilary

Hilary's Journey

I was born in Whitehaven, the oldest of three. My mother was a social worker but became a teacher. My father was a Methodist Minister and that meant that we moved a lot (I was born into itinerant vagabondage!). When I was around 2 we moved to Whitefield in North Manchester; at 5 to Stockport; at 10 to New Mills in Derbyshire; and when I was 16 my parents moved to Widnes. I came to Manchester University in 1977 to study linguistics and French. After graduating in 1981, I did a PGCE in Chester, moving back to Manchester where I bought a house in Ladybarn when I completed. I then travelled to Oldham for the next nineteen years where I taught languages in two different schools. I was assistant head in one of them and then later I moved to Wigan where I was full-time deputy head. In 2008 I stopped teaching and now am an educational consultant for Manchester Metropolitan University and the University of Manchester.

Stuart's Journey

I was born in Mirfield where my parents were both schoolteachers. They met teaching at Mirfield Grammar School. My father continued there when it became a comprehensive. They still live in Mirfield. I am the younger of two sons. I went to Queen Elizabeth Grammar in Wakefield from the age of 9 until 18 and then went to Oxford University. I lived in Oxford from 1980 to 1990, first doing a BA in History at St Catherine's and then a PhD, also in history, at Nuffield College. I taught at New College after that until I moved to Heaton Norris in 1990 when I was appointed to the French Department (initially, as my specialisation was French history) at Manchester University. I transferred to the History Department after four years and now I am a professor there.

I had seen Hilary at Holy Innocents Church in 1991 where she was handing out hymnbooks but also I met her again, later that year, at a French Department Comic Review put on by staff and students. Hilary was brought along by her lodger, an Erasmus student, who was friends with one of the lecturers. I recognised her from church.

We married in June 1992 at Holy Innocents Church. Hilary's house sold first so we lived in my flat in Heaton Norris until we found this house and moved here in 1993.

Hilary and Stuart

We had a very chequered time finding a property. We wanted a place where Stuart could walk to work since I would have had to drive to Oldham anyway. I had already lived in this general area and liked the kind of houses on the street (Edwardian villas) which were similar to ones I had lived in previously on Amherst Road which I also liked. We needed a house big enough to hold our huge collection of books and to host people who would come to stay. We looked around Victoria Park and elsewhere until we saw this one advertised in a window at Reeds Rains Estate Agents.

This house had been occupied by a couple who had kept it in punctilious order. They were extremely security conscious and had bricked up one of the side windows to prevent breach by anyone from the street, and made the other which was in a more secure location so small that no one would be able to fit in. There were fourteen locks on the front and back doors and aggressive planting. Gradually we have worked round the house, replacing doors, windows and restoring the leaded lights. It took us years to get the thorn at the back door fully under control!

It's good being able to cycle to work in five minutes. It's a very nice street; quiet and very well situated. You can get out of Manchester quite quickly. Culturally, it is interesting, and we have excellent neighbours. People look out for each other in a very understated way. It's convenient for buses. They are very nice houses to live in.

RESIDENTS IN 1911	RESIDENTS IN 2019
WILKINSON, Henry Born: 1872 Occupation: Manager Cotton Master Manufac Chorlton on Medlock Manchester Lancashire	Stuart Born: 1962 Mirfield, West Yorkshire Occupation: Academic, Department of History at University of Manchester
WILKINSON, Elizabeth Born: 1871 West Gorton Manchester Lancashire Wife	Hilary Born: 1959 Whitehaven, Cumberland Occupation: Secondary School Teacher
WILKINSON, John Born: 1901 Reddish Manchester Lancashire Son	

Helen

Helen has lived on the street since 1976

Helen

Helen's Journey

I was born in Coventry, in 1948. My parents came from Ireland: Dad from Mayo and Mum from Galway. Dad was a plasterer and Mum came to England during the war. She worked first as a nurse for a short time, returned to Ireland briefly, and then came back to England and worked in a factory. She ended up as a primary school teacher in Coventry. I have one brother and one sister. He lives in Milan and she is a librarian at Warwick University. After art college in Coventry I taught in a local school for a year. Then I applied to St. Pius Xth (later renamed St. Vincent de Paul) on Denison Road in Victoria Park. I came to Manchester to work there in March 1973.

At first I lived in Withington and then Alexandra Road South. I met my future husband, Ben, through a mutual friend in January 1976, and married him in July 1976, seven months later. We didn't hang about! He was a lecturer at the University of Manchester Medical School and had already been living in this house since September 1975, after resigning as tutor and then warden at UMIST's Chandos Hall, a student residence close to the Mancunian Way. Ben was from the East End in London and was born in 1929; his parents were Russian immigrants of Jewish extraction. He had left school at 14 but had always wanted to follow his older brother into education so he studied at night, first getting his O-Levels, then his A-Levels and finally his undergraduate degree from London University, all while working during the day. He then went to Southampton University and after receiving his PhD, came up to the University of Manchester Medical School in 1968 to teach physiology. He remained there until he retired in 1998. After giving up his wardenship he looked for a house that was near to the university and bought this house. He had been here a year when I moved in.

The house had been in multi-occupancy with locks on all the internal doors when he bought it and it became his project, which I joined, to make it into a family home. He was a great believer in DIY and rewired the house, put in central heating, a new hot water tank in the loft, and took down walls to change the room layout amongst other things — entirely on his own. He used girders from an old Anderson shelter to prop up the kitchen ceiling. I remember him loading a girder onto the roof of the car and then seeing the car sink right down on its springs! Once he'd completed his work, I took over and did the decorating.

Rusholme at that time was like a little village with a variety of shops. I remember the baker, fishmonger, butcher, and the Trocadero cinema. I went with a friend to a matinee just before I met Ben. An Indian sweet shop had just opened and our afternoon was a real Bollywood experience, complete with samosas at the interval. Then the second curry house opened up. Ben and I thought it would never survive.

I continued to work at St. Pius Xth until the Catholic schools were reorganised and then at The Hollies in Didsbury until I retired. Both schools have now closed. Our two daughters were born here, both now grown up. They played with the neighbours' children outside in front of the house and on the large tree which still stood in our front garden until relatively recently. The road was very quiet then, with far fewer cars parked on either side. I didn't know too many people because I was working. The street had many long-term residents but also many boarding houses or houses in multiple occupancy. Now the street is much more sociable with lots of activities going on.

In many ways it is hard living in this house now as it has so many memories for me but I feel very comfortable here and safe, particularly since gates have been installed in the alleyway behind my house. My entire married life has been here and I wouldn't want to live anywhere else.

RESIDENTS IN 1911	RESIDENTS IN 2019
WOMERSLEY, Charles Frederick Born: 1886 Manchester Lancashire Occupation: Accountant	Helen Born: 1948 Coventry Occupation: Retired Art Teacher
WOMERSLEY, Ethel Maud Born: 1871 Manchester Lancashire Wife	
GILL, Emily Anne Born: 1893 Masham Yorkshire General Servant Domestic	

Ralf and Lida

Ralf and Lida have lived on the street since 1994

Left to right: Ralf, Sascha, Lida and Gina

Ralf's Journey

I was born in 1956 in Aalen, a small town in Germany, less than 30 miles from the Bavarian border. My father's family had been long established there but my mother had come to Aalen as a refugee from Sudetenland, a German enclave that used to be in the Czech Republic. My grandparents from my mother's side were originally farmers. My grandfather from my father's side was a train driver and convinced monarchist. He had been shot in the head in World War I and got away with criticising Hitler because people thought he was mentally affected by this injury. My father's eldest brother, Uncle Josef, a regional boxing champion, was also opposed to the Nazis' ideology. He confronted an officer and avoided being court-martialled due to his close connection with Field Marshal Rommel, who wanted my uncle to become his driver. My father was lucky enough to be too young to get into the war but all his three brothers had to go. Fortunately they all came back.

My father left school at 15 and became a mechanic. However, he was not enjoying this manual job and soon joined the optical company, Zeiss, where he met Russian scientists fleeing east. Amongst them were grandmasters in chess, who spotted my father's talent, and after a short while his main occupation became playing chess for the company. Many years later, still unhappy with his repetitive and not challenging job, he left the company without notice. By then he was married with four children and we went through a difficult time. This was the beginning of computers entering the work place; government was looking for people with high intellectual abilities to enter this field. In a regional selection test my father came second best out of 1,000 people (with an IQ of 184). After his training in 1965, my father found a system computer programming position with Knorr in Heilbronn (a twin city with Stockport) and we moved there and lived in a spacious company house. I saw computers for the first time when he took me to work with him on Saturday mornings. My mother was a secretary and then a housewife. I was the oldest child in the family with four sisters. I went to Justinus Kerner Gymnasium, a scientifically orientated high school. I received a government grant to go to university. I decided to study physics even though chemistry was my favourite subject, and went to Heidelberg because I was also interested in astronomy and they had an observatory. Then I was conscripted but I refused to join the army. I was recognised by a court as a conscientious objector and instead of going to the army, I worked in a hospital in Heidelberg for sixteen months in the Cardiology Department, helping with taking and analysing ultrasound images. After that, I went back to university to complete my studies and received my diploma (equivalent to a Master's degree in the UK) in 1984. I decided to read for a PhD at the Max Planck Institute for Extraterrestrial Physics near Munich. During my final year of PhD in 1988, in a conference I met Professor David Williams from UMIST, who asked me to join his research group as a postdoc in astrochemistry (modelling interstellar clouds). At UMIST, I shared an office with Lida who was working as a postdoc in the same field.

After various other posts, I am now working for the IT Department at Manchester University.

Lida's Journey

I was born in Tehran, Iran, in 1955, the youngest of four children (one brother and two sisters). My mother's side were wealthy business people originally from Baku, Azerbaijan, bringing mechanical household goods and engineering products from Russia to northern Iran, by the Caspian Sea, in exchange for agricultural products. With the Russian Revolution, and start of the communist government, my great-grandfather fled to Iran with all he could take and became a landowner and farmer in the county of Mazandaran by the Caspian Sea. His son, my grandfather, married my grandmother, from a noble family, in the Mazandaran city of Babol. My mother was their youngest child. My father's family came from Gilan, another Iranian province along the Caspian Sea, and moved to Babol, where my grandfather had a homeware store. My parents married in Babol, and later moved to Tehran, where my father became, in 1951, one of the private secretaries to Dr Mosaddegh, the elected prime minister of Iran. However, with the coup d'état in 1952, my father was briefly imprisoned until Dr Mosaddegh went into internal exile. My father resumed work as a civil servant in different government departments for a while and then took early retirement and started a car business (his father had opened a garage for heavy goods vehicles in Tehran). My mother was always a housewife.

I was very much looking forward to starting school when I was 6, but unfortunately the entry age changed to 7 that year, and so I had to wait another year. After waiting a whole year, I was very keen to finally go to school and so I used to arrive at the school before anyone else at 7 a.m., and wake up the caretaker. Because we lived in the outskirts of Tehran near the mountains, my mother worried about me leaving so early in wintertime with wolves around!

When I was 15 years old, my brother went to Austria to study in Vienna. Three years later when he came home for a visit, I was in my final year of secondary school. My brother said, *'Why don't you come to Vienna and study physics?'* but I wanted to study mathematics with computing. However, one of our neighbours had two daughters, who I knew from school. They were studying in Watford and were visiting their parents and asked me to join them instead. So I came to London in 1974, and went to Watford College for my A-levels and English qualification. I went on to study a

Combined Honours degree in mathematics and computing at Teesside Polytechnic with a few of my Iranian friends from Watford College. I came as an overseas student with the intention to go back home after I finished my degree. However, when I was in my second year, in 1979, the Iranian Revolution happened, followed by the Iran/Iraq war. I completed my degree and asked my parents what I should do next. Unsure about the situation in Iran, I decided to study for an MSc degree in industrial mathematics at Aston University in Birmingham.

With the situation in Iran still unsettled, after my Masters degree in 1982, I started a PhD at UMIST with Professor David Williams. I was very successful with my PhD work, and subsequently was invited to go to Cambridge for a postdoc at the Institute of Astronomy. Following my postdoc position in Cambridge, I had a few offers for research positions in the US as well as in Europe; however, I came back to UMIST in 1988 to continue working with Prof. Williams. In November of that year, Ralf joined our research group and we became very good friends. The following year, I took up a senior lectureship position at Manchester Metropolitan University, School of Computing and Mathematics. We married in 1992 and lived in a flat in Heaton Chapel.

Ralf and Lida

One of Lida's friends had a daughter, Rokhsana, who lived in this house. When she and her family had to move to Didsbury, Rokhsana suggested that we could rent their house until their job situation and other commitments became clear. Initially Ralf was not keen, but we moved in on 31 October 1994, just before our son Sascha was born. In 1996, Gina was born and we started looking for a house to buy. We liked the neighbourhood and decided to look for a house nearby. When we talked to Rokhsana about our decision, she suggested that we could buy their house and so we did, in April 1997.

We feel we have been very lucky to live in this house. We very much like the area, love the parks nearby and are exceptionally happy with our lovely neighbours. It is great that we live so close to our work and had access to the best schools in Manchester for our children.

RESIDENTS IN 1911

CURRIL, John
Born: 1856
Glasserton, County Wigtown
Occupation: Credit Draper

CURRIL, Helen
Born: 1858
Glasserton, County Wigtown
Wife

CURRIL, William
Born: 1891
Manchester, Lancashire
Occupation: Chartered
Accountants Articled Clerk

RESIDENTS IN 2019

Ralf
Born: 1956
Aalen, Germany
Occupation: Information
Systems Manager,
University of Manchester

Lida
Born: 1955
Tehran, Iran
Occupation: Principal Lecturer
and Course Leader for
Mathematics, Manchester
Metropolitan University

Sascha
Born: 1994
Manchester
Student at Warwick University
studying Mechanical Engineering

Gina
Born: 1996
Manchester
Occupation: Studying English,
History, Economics and Maths
at Withington Girls' School

Harry and Katrina

Harry and Katrina have lived on the street since 1998

Left to right: Elizabeth, Harry, Elliot the cat and Katrina

Harry's Journey

I was born at home because my parents couldn't afford to have another baby in hospital. My father, also Harry, was an electrical spot welder at Avro (an aircraft manufacturer), Chadderton, and met my mother, Sarah, there. She had been drafted into war work at Avro's during World War II, and came from South Shields. They met in the air raid shelter. I have a brother, Jeffrey, seven years older than me. I went to Burgess Street Infant and Junior School, to North Manchester Grammar School for Boys and then to Mather College of Education. My parents were both very intelligent but not able to go to grammar school themselves. They did everything to encourage me and my brother. It gave my dad great satisfaction when he realised that he was cleverer than his former schoolmate who turned out to be my maths master. Later on, my mother worked at the Co-operative Biscuit Works in Crumpsall and also as a cleaner. She trained to be an auxiliary nurse at Booth Hall Children's Hospital but never actually was a nurse because she had children.

I could have gone to Plant Hill Comprehensive as comprehensives had just been created but my primary school wanted me to go to the grammar school. I stayed on for Sixth Form. I had applied elsewhere but didn't get in. I was working as a porter at Smithfield Market when a friend said, 'Try Mather.' So I applied there and got accepted to train as a French teacher. I qualified in 1972 and started teaching at Abbot County Primary School in Collyhurst, stayed there a year, and then went to Varner Street Primary in Higher Openshaw for three years. From there I taught at Wenlock Way in Gorton and then at Ashbury in Beswick. I had a brief time at management when I was deputy head teacher at Church of England School of the Resurrection but went back to teaching at Ashbury in 1989. Then the local secretary of NASUWT (National Association of Schoolmasters Union of Women Teachers) retired and I was elected to take his place. I have worked as local secretary ever since, becoming president of Manchester Trades Union Council. I visited Leningrad in 1987 and now I am chair of the Mechanics Centre in the Mechanics Institute where the Trades Union Congress was founded.

In 1971, I got married and moved to Droylsden and lived there until 1994 and had a son. We separated in 1978. In 1994 I met Katrina at an equal opportunities conference at the Union's headquarters. I had been living in a flat but then went to live on Redruth Street, just off Platt Lane, with her.

Katrina's Journey

I was born in Dewsbury Hospital, Yorkshire. My parents had been childhood sweethearts, their fathers having served in the same battalion in the First World War and settling in Filey on the north Yorkshire coast. My dad was the stationmaster at Cleckheaton Station and I spent my first five years of life in Cleckheaton with my dad, mum and my brother and sister, living in the Station House. My mum remembers Mr Beeching knocking at our door, saying that the station was going to close.

Dad got a new job at Wyke as area manager at Bradford Interchange. It was my first experience at being an outsider. Though Wyke was only two villages away, my accent was a bit different, saying 'ey-ut' instead of 'eight'. It took a while to get established. After my brief time at school in Cleckheaton I went to Wyke Infant, Junior and Middle schools and then Wyke Manor Comprehensive. My dad had a serious accident when I was 10 which gave him a brain injury (he fell out of a window) and he was disabled after that and our family life was disrupted. My brother left home and my sister was at university. My mum and I became his main carers.

When I was 19, I came to Manchester Polytechnic to do a history degree and then I took a year off to go back to Bradford to help Mum because Dad had deteriorated. I returned to Manchester Polytechnic and did a PGCE specialising in early years. I lived all over Manchester where students lived – in Didsbury, Ladybarn, Chorlton, Whalley Range, West Didsbury, and then bought a house on Redruth Street, down Platt Lane. I started teaching in 1988 with a job at Stanley Grove, Longsight, as a nursery teacher. I was there for 15 years. I met Harry on 17 March 1994. I was Equal Opportunities Coordinator for Stanley Grove and I spoke to Harry on the phone to get information about going to a conference on the subject, and he gave me a lift to Birmingham. After that he moved to Redruth Street with his son and lived there with me until 1998.

Harry and Katrina

Katrina: I knew Nicky because she worked at Stanley Grove too and Elizabeth who lived across the street from this house was also there. Nicky told Elizabeth we were looking to move since the house on Redruth Street seemed small with only two bedrooms, the City grounds next door, and the last straw was our car being written off, on the street. Elizabeth said, '*You're going to live on my street*', and brought me over here and knocked on the Libby's door (they were living here then) so I could look at it. I got Harry and he looked at it and then we brought friends round to look at it and came and looked again and then we bought it! We loved the house and its original features. It just felt right even though it needed a lot of work. It had a garden and a garage, particularly important to Harry who had been brought up in a two-up-two-down with backyard and outside toilet.

We moved here in March 1998 and had our daughter Elizabeth in 2002. After she was born, I was a supply teacher at many schools in the area and now work at

Collyhurst Nursery School and Children's Centre. We think it is overwhelmingly lovely here most of the time. We love the multicultural character of the street, the mixed economy and the fact that it is in M14. Some of the families of the children I taught live on the street. There can't be anywhere better than Manchester. Elizabeth has enjoyed growing up here and loves our house. The footprint of Harry's childhood house would slot into Elizabeth's bedroom! Our first cat is buried in our garden and now Elliot, a rescue cat, lives with us.

RESIDENTS IN 1911	RESIDENTS IN 2019
MEAKIN, Jane Elizabeth Born: 1853 Bradford Yorkshire Occupation: Private Means	**Harry** Born: 1951 Harpurhey Occupation: Primary School Teacher and now full-time Trade Union Secretary for National Association for Schoolmasters Union of Women Teachers (NASUWT)
MEAKIN, Edith Born: 1878 Manchester Lancashire Occupation: Private Means, Daughter	
RIDGE, Nellie Born: 1887 Cheadle Staffordshire Occupation: Servant	**Katrina** Born: 1964 Dewsbury, Yorkshire Occupation: Teacher (Early Years) at Collyhurst Nursery School & Children's Centre
	Elizabeth Born: 2002 St Mary's hospital, Manchester Schoolgirl (at Trinity High School)

Halimo

Halimo has lived on the street since 1994

Halimo

Halimo's Journey

Both of my parents were born in Hargeisa, which was then part of French Somalia. My father joined the French army in Djibouti, where two of my brothers were born. After the army he bought livestock (sheep, goats and camels) and became a nomadic farmer, moving around a lot, looking after the animals. The family moved around with him. My mother looked after the family. They had eight children, four boys and four girls (but only three are still alive). I was their fifth child. I lived with my grandma in Hargeisa for ten years and then rejoined my family when I was 11. I had no schooling. My parents thought boys go to school; girls have children. I am annoyed about that now! My uncle (my mum's brother) was one of the richest men in Somaliland. He was working in Saudi Arabia then. He took my mum and his other sisters on Hajj and gave them loads of money. He built houses for his mother and his sisters in Hargeisa but my mother went back to the nomadic life with my father. When I was around 11½, my dad decided he wanted a second wife because he wanted more boys. Mum and her friends went out looking for a wife for him and found one and he got married. I wasn't happy about this because he then forgot his first family. It still hurts me, even today.

After a while, Mum came back to Hargeisa and my uncle helped take care of us and brought us up more than my father did. Then my mum suddenly became ill and had to have an operation. Sadly, she died four days after it, so my little sister and I went to stay with my uncle and his wife for about three years. And then I went to my auntie's (mum's sister) to live, and came to call her 'mum'. When I was in Hargeisa I went to night school for about two years. All the girls and boys who didn't go to school when they were younger went if they could, but you had to pay for it.

When I was 17 my auntie's brother-in-law (her husband's brother) came to visit from the UK. He stayed for quite a while and then asked his brother and my auntie if I would marry him. Auntie asked me whether I would agree, would I accept his offer. I was so shy and I said from behind my scarf, '*If you think he's good for me, I will.*' In one week we were engaged and two weeks later we married. I was 17½. It was amazing!

My husband, Elmi (Elmi means knowledge) was born in Berbera also in Somaliland Region in 1930. He was 33 when I married him and had been living first in Saudi Arabia for five years and then in England for the past four years. He stayed with me in Hargeisa for three months and then returned to the UK where he was working as a chef in a Birmingham hospital and applied for my visa. I was thinking I am going so far away and was very scared but after nine months I joined him in Birmingham. We lived in a flat at first with our daughter before buying a house. Within four years I had four children and then later, two more. I thought I would go mad. It was very hard work but it made me a strong person. I was the only Somali girl in the whole city of Birmingham and my English was limited. My husband was working seven days a week. It was so lonely at the beginning. But my husband was an amazing support. He helped me in every possible way. He was everything to me. He cooked, took the children out; he was like a husband, father and friend. We brought our children up in Quinton, Birmingham, and lived there twenty-six years and it really feels like home. I will go back there when I retire. I learned English in the 1970s when my children were in school. They had an English class there. The pupils were all Asian ladies except me.

I started working in school meals at first and then I started looking for another job. I saw an ad for one of Birmingham's famous restaurants and went for an interview. The manager, a Greek guy called George, who was only 25 years old, interviewed me. *'When can you start?'* he said. I was the second oldest person working there. It was amazing and good fun. I worked there for eight years, preparing food. When I left, they had a big party for me.

While I was working there the Somali Civil War started and my sister and my husband's brother came to us from a refugee camp. I was working; my husband was working; the children were in school and college. My sister was very lonely and told us she wanted to go back to Somalia.

'I don't speak English,' she said. *'I am home here by myself. I need to move where some Somali people are or I will go back to Somalia.'*

My youngest sister came too. She had a heart condition and needed an operation. The doctors wouldn't let her go back after that. So we wrote a letter on her behalf and the rest of her family came to join her.

We knew someone in Worsley so we decided to move to Manchester. My husband looked in the papers to find a house and came here on weekends to look around. He saw an ad for this house for £95,000. We bought it in 1994 and paid £90,000 cash for it. A vicar from Platt Church had been living here. Our youngest girl was 14 when we came to Manchester on 8 November 1994 and she went to Parrswood High School. My sister lives in Manchester too now, in Moss Side.

I went to the town hall and found a freelance job with the International Translation Service. I worked for them a while and travelled a lot for them – to Liverpool, Preston, Bolton and Bury – which was really nice. Then I went to the hospital as a freelance, part-time. I got a permanent full-time job with the NHS Trust in 1997 and I am still working there. There is never a dull moment. I do translating and work in the office as well.

Soon after we came to Manchester my husband became unwell. He didn't work in Manchester and was in and out of hospital. I didn't know what was wrong with him and the doctors didn't tell me. When someone gave me a leaflet about leukaemia I was shocked and nearly passed out. On 2 January 1998 he died. I thought there was no life left for me but you just have to live and survive for the children. He was an amazing man.

None of my children live in Manchester now; they live all over England, all married to English partners and all with good jobs. I have twelve grandchildren.

It is amazing here. I couldn't ask for better neighbours on both sides. I feel they are like my family, especially Nicky and Phil. It is so calm here, so quiet, so amazing. I really love it. I love, love, love this street and the people living on it.

RESIDENTS IN 1911	RESIDENTS IN 2019
SCHOFIELD, Eliza Jane Born: 1846 Manchester Widow	Halimo Born: 1946 Somalia Occupation: Translator and Interpreter for the NHS Trust
SCHOFIELD, Bertha Born: 1879 Manchester Occupation: Teacher Elementary School	
SCHOFIELD, Edward Billington Born: 1881 Sale Occupation: Chartered Accountant	
SCHOFIELD, Herbert Payne Born: 1883 Sale Occupation: Insurance Clerk	
SCHOFIELD, James Murray Born: 1885 Sale Occupation: Insurance Clerk	
SCHOFIELD, Elsie Jane Born: 1886 Sale Occupation: At Home	

Phil and Nicky

Phil has lived on the street since 1981 and Nicky since 2003

Phil and Nicky

Phil's Journey

My father worked for Monsanto Chemicals, which was mainly a plastics company then and not involved in bio-engineering. As he moved higher up in management, we moved house, mostly in Wales, to accommodate his new jobs. By the time I was 11, we had moved seven times. Eventually we ended up in Wales, where I went to Newport High School, and I stayed there through Sixth Form. My mother was from Burry Port near Llanelli. She and my father met when they both worked in an armaments factory in South Wales during the war. Although she briefly worked for Seeger's Gin, she was a traditional housewife once I was born. I have one younger brother, Clive.

After high school, I attended Imperial College, London, for five years from 1968 to 1973, getting my BSc in Chemistry and MSc in Biochemistry. I travelled around the USA and Canada for five months in 1974 and then went back to London where I found a few casual jobs (including working at Corona Bottling Company and cleaning operating rooms at the Royal Free Hospital). I was offered several biochemistry jobs in London but I didn't like the London grind. I applied to Manchester Royal Infirmary and came up here in June 1975 to start work researching celiac disease. I liked it in Manchester as it was friendly and easy to get around. I lived with my cousin in a flat just off Barlow Moor Road for a year and met my wife, Elizabeth, in 1976, through some friends of my cousin. She lived with a group of girls on Burton Road. We bought a house on Old Hall Lane in 1977 and got married a few weeks later. It was the Queen's Silver Jubilee year and we were also a 'Liz and Phil', aka 'Fizz and Lil'. Elizabeth was teaching History and RE at Levenshulme High School then. We had our first child, Alexander, in 1979, and then our third, Thomas, in 1981, having lost our second child, Ruth, soon after she was born. Elizabeth discovered this street when she met Elaine (who lived on it) through a playgroup, and liked it so much that she went looking for houses for sale there immediately. I wasn't too happy about moving since I had just done a lot of work on the Old Hall Lane house and I didn't have a permanent job at the hospital then. We went to see the house and after our visit – under great pressure from Elizabeth, who went upstairs to bed in tears (I found her crying under the covers clutching the estate agent's blurb to her bosom) – I agreed that we could put in an offer. The house was owned by two doctors who kept two Alsatian dogs. The back garden was mostly dog kennel and the house was covered in dog hair. It seemed ridiculously huge. But Elizabeth loved it and its Edwardian style and so we bought it. The house cost £28,000 which seemed a lot of money at the time. We sold our house on Old Hall Lane for £10,000. My job became permanent nine years later.

Our fourth child, Mark, was born in 1984 and Liz died in 1999. I stayed on here. Thomas and Mark were still at home but Alexander was at the University of Bristol. Nicky moved here in October 2003 so I've never lived here on my own.

Nicky's Journey

My parents met during the war as conscientious objectors doing relief work. Elizabeth's father was also a conscientious objector but unlike my parents, he was imprisoned in Wormwood Scrubs for his beliefs. Our fathers met while working in the Friends' Ambulance Unit. My father went to Goldsmith's for his BEd and trained as a potter and arts and crafts teacher there. My mother was a Froebel-trained nursery teacher. She loved being a mother but resisted a traditional female role. For most of my childhood I lived in Chatham and then we moved to Bristol where my father worked at the same teacher training college as Elizabeth's father. On Saturday mornings, the college ran a pottery class for children of the staff and I met Elizabeth there in 1962 when we were 9 or 10. We were firm friends from then on. Although we went to different primary schools we later went to the same high school, where we sat together, played cello, laughed and played tricks on people. We lived about 2 miles apart and I used to get up early and cycle or walk to Elizabeth's house, eat breakfast with her and her family and then walk to school with her. I was 20 when I married Les and moved to London and then went to university at Goldsmith's, studying Social Science. After that we moved to Huddersfield so that Les could finish his architecture degree. We had our first child, Annie, in 1978, and then, two daughters later, in 1985, Les got a job with Johnnie Johnson Housing Trust in Bramhall near Stockport. I didn't want to leave Huddersfield but was willing to live in Manchester near Liz and Phil. We took a short piece of string and moved it around their street on the A to Z map ending up close by. I could see Liz and Phil's house from an upstairs window. I was child-minding then and Liz was about to start back to work so Mark came to me to be looked after, along with the other children. Later, I ran Birch After School Club and then in 1989 went to Didsbury Polytechnic to do teacher training. The following year I started teaching at Stanley Grove Primary School. Katrina, who now lives across the street from us, was teaching there then, too, and the children from another house on the street attended school there.

Les moved out in January 1997. We sold our house and I went to live in Burnage. I kept coming back to see Elizabeth, who was ill by then. It was very hard for me as well as Phil after she died. Elizabeth's family had a strong connection with the Lake District and had established a stone bench near Langdale Pikes, which my children found by accident on a previous holiday when we were renting a house in the area. Later, a year after she died, when the time came to scatter Liz's ashes, a party of family and friends rented that same holiday house and we scattered her ashes around the bench.

Nicky and Phil

We stayed in touch, sharing outings to concerts, the theatre or dinner at each other's houses. We will always remember the week we decided to get together as it coincided with an earthquake in Manchester in October 2002, but we didn't live together here until a year later. We like living on this street and like the multicultural mix of people here. Over the years there have been quite a few characters: Mrs Samson, Mrs Donnelly (who used to feed Elizabeth stacks of bacon butties when she was ravenous from steroids, and brought soup and soda bread for the family) and Gay Lewis. It was a friendly place for the children to play in. Being a quiet road made it easy to meet people and added to the sense of community. Nicky was warmly welcomed on the street when she moved here.

RESIDENTS IN 1911	RESIDENTS IN 2019
FOX, Samuel Smith Born: 1828 Manchester, Lancashire Occupation: Resident Assistant Agent	Phil Born: 1950 Llanelli, S. Wales Occupation: Biochemist
LEECH, Ellen Born: 1868 Manchester, Lancashire Occupation: Housekeeper Domestic	Nicky Born: 1952 York Occupation: Retired Teacher/ Children's Services Worker
SMITH, Wilfred Arthur Born: 1888 Witham in HillLincolnshire Boarder	

Elisabet and Abbasi

Elisabet and Abbasi have lived on the street since 2005 (living at another house until 2008)

Left to right: Elisabet, Sara, Abbasi and Haroon

Elizabet's Journey

My father was originally a primary school teacher but moved on to work in a bank. His father was an army doctor so the family lived in many places because of his work until he decided to settle down as a GP in Murcia. My mother was from Murcia and was a nurse. My parents met in Islas Menores when their families were both on summer holiday there. After they returned to Murcia, they continued their relationship and eventually married. I am their oldest child, with one younger brother. I went to school in Murcia and then to university there, too, and graduated with a degree in English language and literature. I spent some time at Salford University in my third year on an exchange and then in my fifth year (2001) returned to Manchester Metropolitan University (MMU) on an Erasmus scholarship and continued studying English language and literature but also German and Spanish. While at MMU I met Abbasi through a mutual friend. I was originally offered a place at Leeds University but asked to transfer to Manchester because of my time in Salford and, when someone dropped out, this was agreed. Abbasi had chosen to come to Salford despite also being offered places in Glasgow and Canterbury. Had that not happened, we wouldn't have met and our lives would have been very different! I returned to Spain to do teacher training so I could be an English teacher in Spain but after that I went back to England to Leeds to get an English Teaching Certificate (to teach Spanish in England) because I wanted to be with Abbasi.

Abbasi's Journey

My ancestors came from Iraq originally; our tribe was the Halifa Al-Abbasi, part of the Abbasi Caliphate which ruled from 750 to 1258 when the Mongols attacked Iraq. The head of the tribe, Ghia Khan, took his people (no more than 200 of them) to what became Abbotabad in the foothills of the Himalayas in what is now a National Forest Preserve.

By the time my father had become a young man he had moved to Karachi. He was a businessman and had several hotels and restaurants throughout the area which he had set up so others could manage – an early version of a franchise. We were a middle-class family with servants.

I had an older brother called Haroon. When we were quite young (ages 3 and 4) my mother took us to see the old village in the mountains, and because he was unused to the cold and because of the primitive conditions there (no electricity, constant snow, and water only available from the mountain streams) he became ill and died of pneumonia. This caused my parents to separate for a while and it meant that I stayed on in the village with my mother for two years.

When I was 5 years old we moved to Islamabad where my father had transferred his business and lived as a family together again. At age 6, I went to Jack and Jill School which was taught in English. I was not happy about it but I learned easily. Although my mother did not speak English my father did. It was a shock to the system moving there after my time in our village – I really did not like learning in English. I was a rural village boy mixing with the sons of middle-class professionals. The experience made me up as a fighter for the under-privileged from a young age. We stayed on in Islamabad and I went to Islamabad Model School where I did O-levels and on to A-levels at H/8 College. All my schooling was taught in English. I was good at sports, particularly football and athletics. In my first race I came last. I didn't like that and practised until I started winning. I wore a t-shirt with '*Catch me if you can*' printed on the back. While I was at H/8 College I was chosen by the Pakistan Ministry of Education as the best male student in Islamabad, to take part in an International Youth Exchange Programme to Canada.

So, at age 18, I went to Port Hoxbury on Cape Breton Island in Nova Scotia where I lived with a Canadian family for a year. Before I got there both I and the local hosts took part in an induction course to learn about each other. This greatly helped me to understand and adapt to local customs and ways of doing things. It meant that when I eventually came to England I didn't move into a ghetto. While I was in Canada I did a work placement and shared in a cultural exchange programme. I returned to Pakistan in 1990 and by the end of 1990 I came to England to continue my education. I would have preferred to go back to Canada or to Australia but my parents wanted me to come to England so I went to Swindon College. There I was advised that it would be a good idea to get English A-levels so I took an access course at the age of 21 and then went on to do a BA Honours at Salford University in TV and Radio. I finished in 1997. Whilst I was studying I also worked part-time at the BBC reporting on Asian Affairs. I went back to Pakistan for a year, but I didn't like it (I had become too English – and now I feel neither English nor Pakistani) and I came back to Manchester. I still had the flat in Victoria Park that I had bought when I was a student. I worked for the City Council, then as project manager for the Prince's Trust, and after that with Blackburn Borough Council as a co-ordinator.

Elizabet and Abbasi

Abbasi: We met through mutual friends. Elizabet was Catholic and I was Muslim but we became good friends. When my dad came to visit he liked Elizabet so much he told me I should marry her – and, I later discovered, told her she should marry me! We married in 2003. I did a funded MBA at the University of East London while Elizabet finished her teaching qualification in Leeds. I went to London for four days a week and spent the weekends in Leeds! We finished our courses at the same time and moved into my flat in Victoria Park. We liked this area and didn't want to move away.

Elisabet: We have lived in Rusholme since 1998. In 2005 we bought another house on the street but sold that in 2008 and moved across the road to this one. It was quieter on this side of the street and we wanted more sun! At one point we thought we would move to Prestbury in Cheshire because there might be better schools there, but we liked it here and it is better to be in a mixed area. It is near the city but it has the feeling of living in the country. It is very quiet and there are three parks nearby.

Haroon

It is nice here because I like my neighbours. I am not lonely. It's nice because there are lots of decorations, plants and fences. I like the way each house has different patterns of roofs and I like my school. We go to Platt Fields three or four times a week and I like that too.

RESIDENTS IN 1911	RESIDENTS IN 2019
WORTHINGTON, John Leigh Born: 1876 Gorton Lancashire Occupation: Incorporated Accountant And Secretary	**Abbasi** Born: 1968 Karachi, Pakistan Occupation: Station Manager, Local Radio
WORTHINGTON, Elizabeth Born: 1875 Gorton Lancashire Wife	**Elisabet** Born: 1979 Murcia, Spain Occupation: Innovation Team Leader (Global Data)
WORTHINGTON, Eric Leigh Born: 1907 Gorton Lancashire	**Haroon** Born: 2005 Manchester Occupation: Schoolboy (St Chrysostom's)
WORTHINGTON, Lawrence Geoffrey Born: 1910 Gorton Lancashire	**Sara** Born: 2016 Manchester
URMSTON, Margaret Ellen Born: 1892 Gorton Lancashire Occupation: General Servant Domestic	

Phil and Helena

Helena and Phil have lived on the street since 1991

Left to right: Nora, Ita, Helena, Phil and Ollie the cat

Phil's Journey

My father was a lecturer in Classics at Keele University when I was born. He was very bright and got scholarships all through his academic career. His father fought in the First World War, was an army chaplain and was evacuated from Dunkirk in World War II. My mother's father was half-Italian and half-English; her mother's mother was half Ukrainian. My parents met as they were both finishing university; my father was in an amateur dramatics play in Suffolk and my mum was in the audience. They met at the after-show party. He was at Cambridge and she was at Oxford doing teacher training after her degree. They married and my father's first job was at Keele and my mum taught at a secondary school in Newcastle-under-Lyme. When I was 18 months old my dad got a job at the University of Ghana so we moved to Achimota near Accra. My younger brother and both sisters were born there but we used to come back to Britain most summers for holidays.

In 1962, my father got a job at St David's College, Lampeter, and we arrived just in time for the worst winter in many years. Lampeter was cut off for weeks and the schools all closed. As children, we had no idea of gloves and coats, having been in primary school in Ghana. I went to boarding school at Wells Cathedral School in Somerset and then followed in my parents' footsteps, going to Keele University to study Geography and Biology. I had a sabbatical year because I had been elected secretary of the student union.

I loved my Master's degree at Wye College in Kent in landscape ecology, design and maintenance, which cemented my determination to work to improve the environment. My first job was with Manchester City Council as a landscape assistant. Initially we lived in Chorlton (which I thought at the time was the pits) but bought a house on Great Western Street on the Moss Side/Rusholme border and got a housing grant to renovate it. My eldest daughter, Merry, was born in 1982 and soon after we moved to Birch Grove. When Merry was 4, I separated from her mother, Seona, both committing to staying in the area until Merry was 14. I met Helena in 1987 in The Welcome pub after a local Labour Party meeting. I was doing community and environmental work and Helena was doing community and women's empowerment work.

Helena's Journey

My mum was born in Kells Bay, County Kerry, Ireland. She went to boarding school in Ireland and got a scholarship to Galway University. She came to England after university to find work. She always wanted to be a writer and had two stories published by Faber and Faber. As a child, and ever since, I have gone back to the family home in Ireland, who made and still make me feel very welcome.

My father was born in Newark, Nottinghamshire. Around the time he was born his parents moved into one of the new council houses; they were really good homes with gardens. My father was born before the 1944 Education Act so he left school at 15 but his brother, born two years later, got to go to grammar school. My grandfather made ball bearings for the war effort and my grandmother worked for Marks and Spencer as a shop assistant. Everyone cycled in Newark. There were enough family members for a cricket team and a brother-in-law (the only one with a different surname) was the wicket keeper. My father was a draughtsman when he left school, then trained Physical Education instructors for a while and became a Redcoat at Butlins in Filey where he met my mother. They got married and lived in North Wales, then London, and I was born in Newark.

My father got a job with the *Daily Mirror* doing children's shows on the beaches in the summer and organising children's competitions. We moved to Woodingdean outside Brighton and my brother was born in 1966 when I was 11½ years old. I was very happy to have a new member of the family. I loved the seaside and the pier at Brighton. I went to the local grammar school for girls and I am still friends with some of my classmates. I went to University College London and studied history. I joined a circus act with a group of students there. We made inflatable mattresses and took them around adventure playgrounds in London. After my degree I got a grant to do a Masters in European Working Class History of Nineteenth-Century Europe. Lots of jobs were around when I finished so I got one at Manchester University with Student Community Action. I lived in a housing co-op in Levenshulme but eventually bought a house with two friends in Rusholme, and met Phil in 1987. By then I had done a spell at Hulme Girls' Project and was the first Women's Officer for Tameside Council.

Phil and Helena

We chose this house after quite a search. We liked the house – it had a big garden – and we liked the street. Sue next door was very keen for us to move here. The house was in two flats then. So we camped in the front room upstairs and reconverted it back into one. All the original features were still here, which was one of the things we liked. Everything was white with blue carpets. We moved in, in March 1991. Ita was just over 1 year old; Nora was born here in August 1992. In 1999 we moved out for three months and painted all the rooms different colours!

Around 2007 we nearly left, but the move fell through and we decided to work hard for this street instead. Helena applied for a grant to put in thirteen street trees and Phil started work with Keep Britain Tidy and we began organising regular street tidy-ups. These things led to the beginnings of the residents' association and a commitment with our neighbours to make our street a stronger community to live in. We've especially enjoyed our neighbourhood days when the street was closed. The girls loved it. It is so easy to get in and out of town, and since the 1990s the city has become much more interesting and happening. One of the things we have been doing for years is to decorate the street trees on Christmas Eve. After all these years the trees are so big we have to stand on ladders! We've been very happy here.

Ita and Nora attended St James' C of E Primary School and then St Bede's College. Merry went to Birchfields Primary and then to Trinity High School. All three of them now live in London.

Nora and Ita

We always used to play on the street with Anne Marie, Naomi, Alec and Amy. We had water fights and a neighbour used to complain! We went swimming in the old school pool – we watched it being knocked down. After that we went swimming at the pool at Manchester Grammar School. We walked to school and went to After School Club along with lots of kids from the street. We fed lots of people's cats! It was a great place being so close to town when we got older. When we come back now, the students on the street seem so young. Before, we always looked up to them.

Ita: I came here when I was very young and don't feel like it's changed much. I remember Mrs Donnelly and her garden; Anna and Lajos who used to feed our cats; Gay Lewis, Sandra Palmer, Sue Morgan, Aeofe and her family. Cleo Sheehan used to babysit for us. There are enough people who have stayed a long time that you get a sense of continuity. We always had the Birch Community Centre and friends across the road. There wasn't such a sense of doing things together before the street trees were planted.

Nora: I was still at home when the street parties started and one time I did Irish dancing with a group of neighbour girls as entertainment when the street party theme was '*We've got Talent!*'

We remember when Manchester City was at Maine Road. You couldn't park as the street was full. You could hear the roar of the crowd. City used to be a part of the street.

Merry

I was 9 when we moved to the street and it very quickly became my home. Now I return regularly with my children, they've picked up the same friendly, local vibe and love coming to see their grandparents and meeting various neighbours for chats and they're beginning to play with a new generation of children on the street!

RESIDENTS IN 1911	RESIDENTS IN 2019
CRAWFORD, Henry Coulson Born: 1876 Scarborough Yorkshire Occupation: Electricial Engineer	**Phil** Born: 1954 Stoke-on-Trent Occupation: Artist and Social Entrepreneur
CRAWFORD, Maude Mary Born: 1883 Northwich Cheshire Wife	**Helena** Born: 1955 Newark, Nottinghamshire Occupation: Wandering Scholar
HOOLE, Sarah Jane Born: 1890 Middlewich Cheshire Occupation: General Servant Domestic	**Merewyn (Merry)** (Not pictured) Born: 1982 Rusholme Occupation: Mother and Primary School Teacher
	Ita Born: 1989 Rusholme Occupation: Management Consultant
	Nora Born: 1992 Rusholme Occupation:Sixth Form Physics Teacher

Sophie and Paul

Sophie and Paul have lived on the street since 2015

Left to right: Adeline, Sophie, Paul and Solomon

Sophie's Journey

I was born in Huddersfield where my parents had come so my dad could finish an architecture degree. He never got it but worked with housing associations on various projects over the years instead; my mum was always involved in caring jobs such as child care and teaching. Mum was born in York but my dad is from Sierra Leone. They lived in London, where my older sister was born, and then came to Huddersfield where my next sister and I were born. I am the youngest by four and a half years. We moved to Rusholme when I was about 1½ for my dad's work. We were family friends with Liz and Phil who lived nearby and my mum would only move to Manchester if they could live near Liz and Phil. Although they didn't get the house they went for on this street, we could see Liz and Phil's bedroom window from our house. That house was bought in haste. We were on a main road, it was in a bad state of repair, and there were burglaries and various problems as a result of being near Maine Road football ground. But it was great for Halloween parties – we even found a skull in the loft (medical students lived there before us). We lived there from 1985 until 1997, when my parents separated and I moved with my mum to Burnage. My oldest sister had left home by then, my middle sister had just started university, and my dad was in Poynton. I went to Birchfields Primary School and then Levenshulme High School.

School wasn't a happy time. I didn't like it. I finished at Levenshulme in 2000 and then went to various Sixth Form colleges and ended up at a residential college in Worcester for visually impaired students where I got my A-levels. In 2003, I went to Sheffield University to study criminology and sociology but very soon decided I wanted to be back in Manchester. I was unable to get on the Manchester course until the following year but after a year on the course in Manchester I realised I didn't like it either so I started again, in 2005. This time I did Classical Studies, which I loved. I decided to live in halls in Manchester so I could meet people, and I did. I lived in Grosvenor Hall, now demolished, by the Aquatic Centre, for a year and then moved back to Burnage with some friends. Mum by that time had moved to here with Phil, Liz having died several years earlier.

Paul's Journey

I was born in London at the Royal Free in Hampstead. My mother's family originated from the East End where they were market traders. Eventually they moved to Golders Green where my mum was born. My dad's mother was a Polish Jew who survived two concentration camps. After the war she moved to the new state of Israel. My granddad on my father's side was a Russian Jew from the Crimea who had a colourful history. At the age of 16 he was arrested for possession of 'seditious' (democratic) political printed materials and was exiled to Siberia via the Trans-Siberian Express as an *enemy of the state*. He wasn't permitted to return home but eventually he was permitted to leave Siberia. Because he had contracted TB he went to Switzerland to recover, up in the mountains. After he got better he wound up in what was then British Occupied Palestine where he was a driver for the army. He stayed on when the State of Israel was formed and met my grandma there. They lived on a kibbutz in the north where my dad and his siblings were born and grew up. He passed away before I was born.

My mum worked in the City in various jobs. One was working for a travel agency, which meant she travelled quite a lot. She went to Israel on one of these trips, met my dad and then he moved to England to be with her. They lived in Golders Green in a house similar to these on this street for a year but when my little brother was on the way, they moved to Edgware. Mum often worked, but not full time after she had children. She worked in a Health Care Trust in Barnet. My dad's qualifications (he had gone to technical college in Israel) were not recognised here at first so he did all sorts of things. He was a mini-cab driver; he had a garage where he made wooden toys to sell at markets; and had a series of engineering jobs.

I always played music at school and was good academically. I got a guitar when I was 14 but I'd already been playing through school, playing in some little bands. My flute teacher, a great jazz musician, ran jazz courses in Highgate so I started to go there. At 16, I joined a fantastic band called 'The Wise Wound' who were all older than me. We played at Glastonbury when I was still at school. By the time the band was winding up I felt I was meant to play music. I sat my A-levels where music went well and applied and auditioned for a music course at several places, the best of which was at Salford. I didn't get in so I did another A-level, reapplied and did get in. I moved up in September 1997 and lived in halls. I graduated in 2000 with a degree in Popular Music and Recording. I had my own band and ran a music production business with a friend. It was all happening in Manchester so I stayed on, and I still think, '*this is the place I want to live*'. I started out on Frodsham Street (in Rusholme) for three years before moving into many other places around South Manchester. I got a job with Johnny Roadhouse Music and worked there for the next seven years and did other things on the side (as musicians do). I taught guitar and played covers and functions gigs, did sound engineering for live gigs, and mimed for TV. I met Sophie at the Star and Garter on Fairfield Street around 2001. The Star and Garter is a former Victorian Hotel turned pub and music venue, one of the last that is independently owned and run. It's a home for indie and alternative music and culture so it's no surprise we both ended up there.

Sophie and Paul

Paul: We had a lot of mutual friends, were often in the same places and became good friends quite quickly, hanging out together while Sophie was at Grosvenor and working for the Thirsty Scholar and I was working six days and five nights. We both got off work late and would meet up and get a bite to eat. When she worked at Blockbusters we watched a lot of free films.

We were very good friends for several years but by 2005 we both realised we wanted to be together. I left Johnny Roadhouse in 2007. I was doing a lot with music but not enough for it to be my whole career so I got a job at Salford University as IT and Library Support and stayed for five years. But there was no chance for progress there so Sophie found me a one-year maternity cover with MIMAS, then attached to Manchester University (but no longer), and I stayed with them ever since. Now my job is permanent.

Sophie: In 2005, I was just starting my degree in Classical Studies and living in Burnage. Paul was in West Didsbury. We moved in together in the Burnage house in 2007 and were there until 2010, the year we bought our house at 100 Parrswood Road and got married. Ade May was born in 2013 and Sol was actually born at home in 2015. We were very happy on Parrswood Road but it was small for a long-term family home. While visiting my mum in 2013 we noticed a house two doors away was for sale and tried to arrange for a viewing. There were problems as they seemed to have a buyer and then not have a buyer, so we didn't get anywhere. In 2015, after Sol was born, we decided to look again. This house still hadn't sold and so we tried again for it. We sold our house within two weeks and after a great deal of 'ifs and buts' and last-minute dramatics, finally we got it. We exchanged contracts on 22 October (when it was an auspicious day for the buyers of the Parrswood house).

Now we are staying with Mum and Phil until we get repairs made. We know we will love being on this street. We already do. One of the big drives for moving was that the house is close to work for both of us. It is also close to the children's nursery and Sophie's mum. It's a pretty street; very peaceful and feels like home. We needed more space and we have cut a huge amount of commuting time from our lives.

RESIDENTS IN 1911	RESIDENTS IN 2019
No Entry	**Paul** Born: 1978 London Occupation: Services Support and Development Officer for JISC, and Musician **Sophie** Born: 1984 Huddersfield Occupation: Student Recruitment and Widening Participation Coordinator, University of Manchester **Adeline** Born: 2013 Wythenshawe, Manchester **Solomon** Born: 2015 At Home, Withington, Manchester

Austin and Michaela

Austin and Michaela lived on the street from 2013 to 2015

Left to right: Austin, Marta and Michaela

Austin's Journey

I was born in Amersham. Both my parents were secondary school teachers in Religious Studies. I have one sister who is seven years younger than I am. I lived in Amersham all my life, attending St Clements Danes Comprehensive, until I went to Cambridge University to study History and Philosophy from 1989 to 1992. I travelled around quite a lot after that, spending two years in France and Germany studying more Philosophy as well as German and French (I was in Tübingen and then at the Sorbonne). I returned to Oxford in 1992 to work for my PhD, teaching in Derby from 1997 to 1999 while I finished it. In 1999, I started at Leeds University but went on research leave (mostly spent in Germany) for eleven years, working in four different countries between 2001 and 2005: Austria (Vienna), Italy (Florence), Germany (Berlin, Erfurt and Frankfurt/Oder) and the USA (Los Angeles). These were for various postdoctoral positions but I spent the seven years between 2005 and 2012 teaching in Germany. I was researching German Social Philosophy, really Social Thought and the History of Social Thought. All this time Leeds kept my position there open for me. I met Michaela in 2008 in Berlin at a mutual friend's birthday party. We moved in together in Berlin just before Marta was born.

Michaela's Journey

I was born in the Black Forest area of Germany. The families of both my parents had lived there for many generations. My father was a mechanic for agricultural machines. He died in 2002. My mother worked in a bank until I was born and then was a housewife. I went to a local Gymnasium (Grammar School) called Gymnasium Schönau. I have one sister who is two years younger than I am. She is still living in the area.

After Gymnasium, I had a gap year and travelled in India for a year. I was always interested in travel because my home town was so small. I volunteered in a school in Kerala and travelled around. As a result I became interested in anthropology. I started at the University of Tübingen in 1993 and studied Anthropology and Comparative Literature. I spent an undergraduate year abroad in the USA in Connecticut at Yale University, graduated in 2000 with an MPhil, and then came to Manchester to the Graduate Centre for Visual Anthropology and did another Masters, this time in Visual Anthropology (Documentary Film Making). It was then the only place in Europe that did it. I lived at 376 Upper Brook Street (that's why I wanted to come back to this area!). I graduated in 2002 and moved back to Germany, to Berlin, and worked in TV for a year but I didn't like it. So I started a PhD at Halle in Germany.

I moved around a lot doing field work in Croatia and travelled around following the professor who was my advisor. I finished my PhD in 2008 around the time I met Austin and continued working in Halle as a lecturer in anthropology. I lived in Berlin, but commuted an hour each way, until Marta was born in 2011.

Austin and Michaela

Michaela: I took five months maternity leave and then, as we are allowed to share parental leave in Germany, Austin took the rest of it so I could take up an offer for a postdoc in Italy. We moved to Bologna and lived there for nine months until August 2012. Then we had to separate for a little while because I got a Postdoctoral Fellowship at Harvard that I couldn't turn down and Leeds couldn't hold the job for Austin any longer. Marta and I moved to Boston and Austin went back to Leeds, detouring to Berlin to give up the flat there.

In August 2013, I was offered a three-year position at Manchester. While I was in Cambridge (USA) I saw an advertisement on the internet to rent this house and phoned Austin to go and have a look. He did and liked it. We decided to live here and Austin would commute to Leeds.

Austin: We have been here since September 2013. We really like the street and the area a lot. We like the location. It is urban but so leafy and quiet, just birdsong. Marta likes seeing the boys playing in the street. She is attending Busy Bees Nursery in Fallowfield. The owners are planning to sell the house in the summer so we will be sorry to have to leave.

RESIDENTS IN 1911

GARDNER, Harold Hanby
Born: 1881
Chorlton on Medlock
Manchester Lancashire
Occupation: Estate Agent

GARDNER, Florence A E
Born: 1885
Ardwick Manchester
Lancashire
Wife

GARDNER, Ada D
Born: 1904
Greenheys Manchester
Lancashire
Occupation: School

RESIDENTS IN 2014

Austin
Born: 1970
Amersham
Occupation: Lecturer in
Sociology at Leeds University

Michaela
Born: 1973
Häg, Germany
Occupation: Lecturer in Social
Anthropology at the
University of Manchester

Marta
Born: 2011
Berlin, Germany

Cécile and Rob

———⊱⊰———

Cécile and Rob have lived on the street since 2009

Left to right: Ella, Cécile, Rob and Maggie

Cécile's Journey

My mum and dad live in south-west France. Maman was the second child from a farming family and my papa was born in the adjacent Département Charente Maritime. They met when they both had summer jobs at camps, which were set up so that children from poor backgrounds could have a holiday. Later, Maman became a teacher and Papa worked for a bank. They moved to a village called Blanzac and we (my parents and my younger brother and I) lived in a flat there supplied by the state until I was 10 years old. (If you were a state employee you could live for free in such a house if one was available.) It was located under the town hall, which was built on a slope so that our garden was behind the building and our apartment took up the whole of the town hall footprint. Many years later Rob and I got married in that same *mairie*. I walked to primary school with Mum, who was teaching there. The school was next door to the old castle, which was up the hill from the town hall, so we walked 'from the town hall to the castle' every school day. I have so many nice memories of those times. My granddad would hunt foxes because they killed the local chickens. He would smoke them out. Once a baby fox came out and no one wanted to hurt it so they gave it to Mum who took it to school, and after that we kept it for a pet.

When I was 10, we moved to a house on the outskirts of Voulgézac, a small village 8km away. My dad had been doing it up over the weekends and holidays for the previous six years. My brother and I went on holiday to see my grandparents as we usually did in the summer and when we came back we moved into the new house. The move left me totally isolated and is the main explanation for me being an avid reader. But it also coincided with me starting high school, and as the high school was in the old village I commuted there with Mum and on Wednesdays (when primary schools were closed) my dad took me. At the age of 15, in 1991, I went to the *Lycée de L'image et du Son* in Angoulême (which specialised in cinema studies and graphics and had only opened two years earlier). It had a modern 200-metre long open space with classrooms on two floors on either side. There were palm trees planted in the open space. I didn't stay there to finish my 'Bac' because I wanted to do three languages so I went to another school in Barbezieux where my dad was working, leaving my friends behind.

I left home and went to Bordeaux for three years at the *Classe Préparatoire* (a branch of a Lycée) which would prepare you for getting into *École Normale*, a highly academic school in Paris. If you passed an exam you could continue your education there if you wished; otherwise you could finish after a further year at university. I didn't particularly want to go to the *École Normale*, but you got a good general education at the *Classe Préparatoire* without specialising too much. I studied English and American

Studies and met lots of interesting people. It was very intense (but worth it as I had superb English teachers) with eight or nine hours of classes a day and lots of homework as well. There was a high drop-out rate. My year started with two classes of fifty pupils and at the end there were two classes of twenty-five. I did take the exam for the *École Normale* but didn't pass it (even though I got the second best grade in the country on translation from French into English). Instead, I attended Bordeaux University for my final year, which was easy after the *Classe Préparatoire*!

I applied for an Erasmus year as I was doing finals. There were six places I could have gone to, all in the UK, and I chose the University of Sussex in Brighton because I had met someone in Bordeaux who was on an Erasmus year and came from Brighton. I had never flown before but a friend had just got his pilot's licence so he took me for a 'ride' above the Bassin d'Arcachon, at sunset. Then two days later I flew (on a scheduled flight) to Brighton. It was just after Princess Diana had died, which was the day Rob had come back from Uganda. The international students had come a week earlier than the British students so I was already in residence in my university accommodation when Rob arrived and moved into the adjoining room. I met him the day he arrived, we realised when we later pieced our chronology together.

Rob's Journey

My mother is from Liverpool. Her parents were of Irish and Scottish heritage and the family was involved with shipping but both her parents became teachers. She went to a high school that was twinned with Paul McCartney's and then to Oxford. My dad was born in Southampton but spent his childhood in Bath. His parents were from East London and Dorset. He went to a school in Bath, where his dad was a head teacher, and then to Cambridge. They were both VE Day babies. After they graduated, they both went to Africa in a programme called 'Study and Serve'. It involved studying for a Master's degree while teaching in a university in East Africa. It was an exciting time with all the post-colonial independence movements. Mum went to Tanzania and taught education and Dad went to Uganda to teach agriculture. They met out there and met again when they'd both come back, this time in Barnsley bus station. They married in 1975 and moved to Manchester. Mum taught a variety of subjects at Whalley Range High School at first and later at Xaverian College whilst Dad worked in town planning at Manchester Town Hall and later in Rochdale where he was Head of Policy at Rochdale Town Hall. They lived in Ladybarn and then, from 1976, in Victoria Park, not far from this street, where I was brought up.

My younger sister and I were both born at St Mary's Hospital and went to St Chrysostom's Primary School and then Trinity High School. Before university I went to Uganda for a gap year. My parents returned to Africa for the first time since they had left, to visit me there. When the year was over I returned to Manchester for a week and then went on to Sussex University where I met Cécile in the room next door to mine.

Cécile and Rob

Cécile: After my Erasmus year, I moved back and forth between France and England in order to complete a French Teacher Training course and do my probationary year there so I would be qualified to teach in France. Rob finished his undergraduate degree and got a job in Sheffield and I taught at Sheffield University for a while. We got married in 2003 during one of the periods I was living in France. Rob moved to Manchester and started accountancy training. I joined him in his flat in Chorlton when I had completed my teacher training.

We bought our first house on Birch Hall Lane on the Anson Estate later in 2003 and immediately got two cats. We had looked on this street when we first were planning to buy because I sensed that there was a strong sense of community here and, being an ex-pat, that was very important to me, but nothing was available that we could afford.

Rob: When I was a child most of my friends, who I had met at Birch Community Centre playgroups, lived on this street so I was very familiar with it and already knew many of the people who lived here. When our house got too small (we had Ella by then) and we started thinking about moving to a bigger one, Sandra, an Australian family friend who also lived on the street at the time, rang to tell us that this house was going to be sold and that if we got there quickly we could get it before it went to an estate agent. It was 7 March (the anniversary of our getting together) and we came down to see it and afterwards went to see Elaine down the road (another family friend) who was very pleased that we could be neighbours. It took us a while to sell our house but it finally went through when we were in France for the summer. On our return we packed up and moved in, September 2009. Gay Lewis had lived in this house for approximately fifty years and lots of things hadn't changed, which we liked! For example, it had the original servants' bells, stained glass, a big garden and lots of character. It was funny, too, because we brought the thirty-year old TV which we had been given by the Sheehans who used to live next door almost back to where it had come from. We can see Elaine's house when we look out the window. Imagine, we have been all over the world and ended up in sight of my childhood. The girls go to the community centre and the local schools, and Cécile is a teacher in the city, too.

Cécile and Rob: We like this neighbourhood. It is very green and full of trees and you can hear birdsong because the gardens and surrounding alleyway are full of birds and insects. Birch Hall Lane was more like a desert for wildlife. Maggie was born a year after we moved in. A striking number of households have dual nationality couples and in several neither is English. We fit right in.

We had done a bit of work on the house when we moved in and recently have started updating it into an 'eco-house' while preserving the original features. We are interested in retrofitting older houses and we volunteered for a scheme in 2014 which enabled us to adapt it to reduce energy use by 40 per cent whilst still keeping the house warm enough for Cécile's Gallic expectations. All the walls are now insulated, the under floor too, we have double or triple glazing throughout and solar panels are installed.

Ella

I like it here because I have lots of friends on the street. I don't remember living anywhere else.

RESIDENTS IN 1911	RESIDENTS IN 2019
PEACOCK, George Born: 1878 Nottingham Nottinghamshire Occupation: Manufacturer's Agent Lace	Robert Born: 1978 St Mary's Hospital, Manchester Occupation: Accountant
PEACOCK, Beatrice Born: 1881 Loughborough Leicestershire Wife	Cécile Born: 1976 Ste. Marie, Angoulême, France Occupation: Language Teacher
PEACOCK, Jack Noel Born: 1907 Manchester Lancashire	Ella Born: 2006 Manchester Occupation: Pupil at St James C of E Primary (and artist)
PEACOCK, George Alan Born: 1910 Manchester Lancashire	

WINTERS, Edith	Maggie
Born: 1893	Born: 2010
Thringstone Leicestershire	Manchester
Occupation: General Servant	Occupation: Pupil at St James
Domestic	C of E Primary (and writer)

Zeb

Zeb moved to the street in 1989, leaving in 2010 and returning in 2016

Zeb and Benjamin

Zeb's Journey

My parents came to the UK together from Chittagong in Bangladesh looking for work and settled in Ordsall, Salford. When I was young my father drove a fork-lift truck in a local factory warehouse. I am the third oldest of four brothers and two sisters. I went to Edgerton Primary School and then to Ordsall High School, but we moved to Grandale Street in Rusholme during my first year there. I went through both Lower and Upper Schools at Ducie Central High and then on to Shena Simon College in town. I took A-levels in Chemistry, Biology and Physics and then a degree in Chemistry at Manchester Metropolitan University. I took two postgraduate diplomas at UMIST – Petrochemical and Hydrocarbon Chemistry and then Instrumental and Analytical Science. All the way through I worked at whatever jobs I could find during evenings and weekends to pay my way through.

After leaving university I worked for IBM in Sale for eight months but the work was boring and I went to work in a laboratory in Leigh. There I met my business partner and she suggested we set up in business together. We decided to go for it in 1999 and the following year set up in Bolton. Two years ago we bought our own building in Trafford Park. There we have been able to set up a bigger testing facility where we carry out physical and chemical testing for fire resistance on furniture, aircraft, car and train parts and fillings. We also test materials on contract, do work for the NHS and even test candles!

In 1989, while I was at Ducie, we moved into the house next door to this one where my mother and sister still live. In 2002 I bought this house and let it out and went to live in Levenshulme. I moved back in here in 2016 and I'm now doing up the house a room at a time. My son, Ben, is now five and going to school in Glossop where he spends time with his mother and the weekends with me.

The street has always been really welcoming with friendly neighbours. We've never fallen out with anyone or had neighbour problems. It is a lovely place to live.

RESIDENTS IN 1911	RESIDENTS IN 2019
BURKE, Kenneth Born: 1868 Decca India Occupation: Journalist	**Aurangzeb (Zeb)** Born: 1973 Salford Occupation: Operations Director of testing laboratory
BURKE, Annie Born: 1871 BanffshireTomintoul Wife	**Benjamin** Born: 2013 Glossop, Derbyshire Occupation: Reception class at primary school
BURKE, Kenneth Born: 1900 Dundee	
BURKE, Murdoch Born: 1904 Dundee	

Ian and Kim

Ian has lived on the street since 2001 and Kim since 2005

Left to right: Ian, First Son, Daughter, Kim, Second Son

Ian's Journey

I grew up in a small, beautiful, remote village just below the tree-line in Teesdale, near Barnard Castle. I knew every one of the 250 residents. I lived there until I went to university. My father owned the village garage and my mother was a tax officer. Her family originally came from a County Durham farming family and my father's from a mining family. They lived within half a mile of each other in a small, tight community. I have an older sister who still lives in County Durham.

I went to Barnard Castle School as a day boy and stayed there until I went to Birmingham University to study Metallurgy and Material Sciences. From there I went to Cambridge to read Theology and then on to Durham University for a second degree. I was ordained in 1981 and was a curate in Darlington and then in Barnard Castle. My first parish was in Teesdale, 5 miles away from where I was brought up, also a very rural and beautiful place with a population of 6,500. In 1990, I became a full-time prison chaplain in the maximum security prison at Full Sutton, York, England's largest. It was a half a mile from where the Battle of Stamford Bridge took place. I stayed there until 1997 and then became chaplain at Manchester University. In 1998, I added on the rectorship of St Chrysostom's while remaining University Chaplain. Now I am full-time at St Chrysostom's and honorary chaplain to the universities. I was made Honorary Canon and Area Dean in 2008. I moved into this house when it became the vicarage in 2001. Kim was a parish assistant about the time I came to Manchester so we knew each other then but didn't get married until much later.

Kim's Journey

My father was headmaster at a local village school and my mother was a teacher. I have two younger siblings. We went to our local county primary school and then to the local comprehensive, Lymm High School. I studied Theology at Manchester University and was parish assistant at St Chrysostom's for a year in 1999 when I met Ian. I went to Birmingham University after that and did an MPhil in Theology whilst training for the priesthood. I was a curate in Rochdale in 2002 after I was ordained and then in 2004 I became Chaplain of the Manchester Universities (which included the University of Manchester, Manchester Metropolitan University, the Royal Northern College of Music and UMIST before it merged with the University of Manchester). Ian and I met again in 2004 when I was at St Peter's Chaplaincy and was living in Chorlton. We married in Jersey in 2005 and we've holidayed there ever since — it has become a special place for us now. I became chaplain at Salford University in 2006, the year our first child was born and in 2009 became assistant priest at St Chrysostom's as well.

Ian and Kim

It is a requirement that the rector of St Chrysostom's live in the parish. But because there were no houses in the parish that were suitable, the Diocese started looking a bit further afield. They had checked out another house on this street but it wasn't in good enough condition and then they discovered that Anna, who lived here, was planning to move. They bought her house instead, without it going onto the market. It was about 5 metres outside the parish so it was necessary to get special dispensation first! The house is a bit small for a vicarage but we've added a downstairs toilet and made other adaptations so it works for us.

Kim: Ian has been living here ever since 2001. I moved in after we married and we had our three children here at the house (each one in a different room and each one in a different season – one in snow, one in spring and one in autumn!).

Ian: It strikes me that we get a different perspective on our area than the other residents of the street as we tend to look eastward, toward St John's school, which is 95 per cent Muslim, and to our church where twelve to fifteen different languages are spoken in the congregation. I am always struck how I can walk a few hundred yards and come to severe urban deprivation. People who come to the church range from university lecturers to people sleeping on the street. I have been through a range of ministries and have always enjoyed working with people on the margins. At St Chrysostom's we welcome a wide range of people including refugees, LGBT people, people with mental health problems and prisoners.

We are very appreciative of our Victorian ancestors, living here: the trees they planted; the walls they built which soften the landscape; the peace and sense of history among all the crowds and action and the multicultural welcome from Victoria Park, one which goes back to its early days with a strong German and Jewish presence. We appreciate our community, the neighbourhood, the Birch Community Centre and more and feel very much a part of two overlapping communities – the parish to the east and this street and beyond to the west. The only thing missing is a corner shop!

RESIDENTS IN 1911	RESIDENTS IN 2019
PRESTON, Annie Born: 1851 Clapham Yorkshire Private Means	Ian Born: 1956 Sedgefield, County Durham Occupation: Rector of St Chrysostom's
PRESTON, Rebecca Born: 1855 Clapham Yorkshire Sister, Private Means	Kim Born: 1977 Lymm, Cheshire Occupation: Chaplain at Salford University
ATKINSON, Dorothy Born: 1890 Dundee	**First Son** Aged 8 Born: At Home, Manchester
	Second Son Aged 6 Born: At Home, Manchester
	Daughter Aged 4 Born: At Home, Manchester

Bibi

Bibi has lived on the street with her family since 1989

Left to right: Shahanara, Bibi and Ashib

Bibi's Journey

I was born in a village near Chittagong in Pakistan (now Bangladesh) in around 1951. My mother came from a wealthy family. They kept many animals in their fields: cattle, sheep, goats and more than fifteen pairs of water buffalo to plough their fields and provide milk. This milk was for the family to drink or share, not to sell. Her family kept their silver coins in copper pots and buried them – there was no bank. In those days people fed each other. They would give poor people rice and chicken; farmers gave food out and helped people who needed it. On my grandfather's and father's land there were vegetables of every kind and all the kinds of fruit trees you could imagine: date, banana, ber (or Indian plum), guava, mango, lychee. The ponds were full of fish. There weren't so many people around in those days. Now there are too many people and they fight for everything. My Nanna died when she was very young and my grandfather married again. Six months after he married, he also died, so my mum went to live with an uncle and her sisters with other members of the family. When she got married she was carried to her new house on a palanquin.

My father was the son of a priest who ran a madrasa. The madrasa is still there.

I married in March 1969. My husband was already living in England; he had come over in 1964. Lots of people had come in 1930, helped by a man called Scottish Ali. Women came too but they didn't stay because it was too cold and uncomfortable for them; they went back. In May 1969, two months after our marriage, we came to Salford. (At that time women followed their husbands whether or not they wanted.) At first we lived near Ordsall Park. Two years later we moved to St James Street, on the other side of the park. There were lots of good neighbours those days – Jimmy, Betty Davies and Samantha – and they chased people away if they came to trouble us. We were the only Asian family. Other good neighbours helped us too: Winnie, Lorraine and Jenny. The children would come round to our house and eat curry and stay all night. We didn't have a bathroom in the house; there was a tin bathtub outside which we had to fill with warm water. There was no electricity; we had oil lights. But when the coalmen went on strike it was particularly hard; there was nowhere to dry nappies. The council demolished a lot of the houses in the neighbourhood then and left many houses empty. Some of the kids would play in them and light candles. There were fires and children died.

I used to miss my home and would cry and cry. I was lonely and it was so cold. In the winter there was snow and everywhere white as a ghost and no one to talk to. I couldn't speak much English; I was very lonely. My sister-in-law, who was here too, went back to Bangladesh in 1974.

In 1984, we moved to Grandale Street. It was a little better and I was a little happier. I was busy taking care of my children, washing, cleaning and cooking. We couldn't stay on Grandale Street because it was too small so my husband went looking everywhere. He found this one. It was in student flats. After a year the owner sold it to my husband.

I had six children but very sadly, one died. Five were born in Salford and the other in Rusholme. In Rusholme, the children went to Heald Place Primary School and Ducie High School and Levenshulme High School. They were brought up like the English kids. In Salford there had not been many Asian families. We were an educated family back in Pakistan and the children have done well here. Most of them have one or two degrees – in chemistry and other subjects.

This street is all right. There is no trouble on the street. On Grandale, there was a little trouble. Here it is a normal street. I knew Mrs Donnelly and Mrs Lewis and Anna and Frank – he was very sociable. It is more multicultural here now. I think Rusholme is fine. It is better now than before.

RESIDENTS IN 1911	RESIDENTS IN 2019
No Entry	Bibi Born: 1951 Near Chittagong, Pakistan (now Bangladesh) Occupation: Housewife Shahanara Born: 1982 Salford Occupation: Laboratory Technician Ashib Born: 1979 Chittagong, Bangladesh Occupation: Catering Assistant

Student House (3)

The household lived on the street from 2015 to 2017

Left to right: Jamie, Samson, Harry, Adam and Monty

Jamie's Journey

My mum is from Birmingham and was an accountant; my dad is from Dublin and is a financial advisor. My parents met at work at an accountancy firm. I have a younger sister still at school. We moved to Horsham where I went to prep school and then to a boarding school in Brighton for four years. I did psychology at A-level and liked it. Manchester was a good university and I wanted to go somewhere different from the South. I lived in Whitworth Park Halls opposite the hospitals on Oxford Road in my first year and my housemates and I got to know each other there. We were all living there except Harry who we met through a mutual friend, so all seven of us applied together. One of us knew the previous tenants and that they were moving out because they had lost some of their housemates and couldn't afford the rent. So we moved in!

Oliver's Journey

I was born in Preston; my dad's from Preston and my mum's from Blackburn. She was a nurse then but now she's a teaching assistant. My dad is commercial director at BAE, working for the military. I've got an older sister who is 21. When I was 4, the family moved to Saudi Arabia but we returned to England when I was 10 because of Al Qaeda. Five years ago we went back, so I've lived nearly half my life there. My mum and dad are there now. I went to primary school in Saudi but went to high school in England in Lytham St Anne's and then boarding school in the Ribble Valley for Sixth Form. I did business, economics and music technology at A-level but I didn't want to do music at university. I knew Manchester well so I didn't really look at other universities. It's a good university and Manchester is a great city – you can't beat it! It's like home from home for me here, so it's worked out well. I am used to living in different places and enjoy it, so it's no trouble going back and forth. The course is OK, but I am not really academic and don't really enjoy it – its bearable! I'm looking forward to finishing and getting a job. In fact, I work part-time at a recruitment firm in town.

Harry's Journey

My dad is from Newton Abbot in Devon and my mum from Portsmouth. They met through their work. Dad is a pharmacist and Mum's a dispenser. I was brought up in Havant about 10 miles from Portsmouth and have lived there since I was 1. My parents are semi-retired now but still do pharmaceutical work part-time. I have two older brothers. One is 26 and is in Norway doing chemical engineering and the other is in Jersey doing his second foundation year of medicine. I went to school in Chichester, all the way through. I chose Manchester because I liked the city; there's a lot going on; it's very diverse; it was somewhere new and it is one of the finest universities. I did maths, physics and chemistry at A-level but was not sure what I wanted to do. Chemical engineering gives me lots of options, pays well, and there are lots of career options – oil and gas, nuclear, pharmaceuticals. I was in Oak House in Fallowfield my first year and joined in with this group through a mutual friend who I knew at Sixth Form. I'm a lifeguard at the Aquatic Centre and like to play football.

Dave's Journey

My father is a Professor of Physics at the China University of Petroleum at Quingdau campus and my mother a lecturer in Engineering. I am an only child. I was brought up in Shandong Province and went to Shandong University for my first two years studying physics. I had lots of choices where I could have gone, but decided to come here for my final two years which will give me an MA (it was part of a connected programme between my university and Manchester) because I liked the course. When I came I lived in Whitworth Park and moved in here with friends I met there. I'm planning to do a PhD after I finish at Manchester, maybe at Cambridge. It's not definite where yet. I like Manchester and doing physics here – it's very cool actually! I like the house and the street.

Jamie, Oliver, Harry and Dave

We like the street and we like the lack of traffic. There are no boy racers. It's a nice area; a good street and a good house. We didn't need to look around. It is different from most student places; it's quiet – not a student area. You can get work done. We've been to other friends' houses in Fallowfield – they're not as nice as this.

RESIDENTS IN 1911

WOOD, Frank
Born: 1856
Manchester Lancashire
Surgical Instrument Maker

WOOD, Edith
Born: 1852
Manchester Lancashire
Private Means

WOOD, Amy
Born: 1862
Manchester Lancashire
Private Means

WRAY, Emma
Born: 1880
Leeds Yorkshire
Occupation: General Servant
Domestic

RESIDENTS IN 2016

Jamie
Born: 1995
Crawley, West Sussex
Occupation: Undergraduate
at Manchester University in
Psychology

Samson

Harry
Born: 1995
Chichester, West Sussex
Occupation: Undergraduate
at Manchester University in
Chemical Engineering

Adam

Monty

Oliver
(not pictured)
Born: 1995
Preston, Lancashire
Occupation: Undergraduate
at Manchester University in
Business and Economics

Dave
(not pictured)
Born: 1992
Quingdau, Shandong Province,
China
Occupation: MA student in
Physics at Manchester
University

Benny

Benny has lived in his flat since 1976

Benny

Benny's Journey

I was born on my parents' farm in Northern Ireland and came to Manchester to work when I was 14 years old. I came straight to this street and stayed with my uncle in his flat for seven years, after which I took it over in my own right. My father died of a brain haemorrhage in 1990.

I went straight into construction and worked as a kerber in road construction for many years until I retired. I met my wife in Manchester, we married in 1990 and she moved into the flat. We had four children – two boys and two girls. Our second daughter was born with holes in her heart and was transferred from St Mary's down the road to Alder Hey Children's Hospital outside Liverpool. While they were operating to give her a heart transplant, my wife went into labour and she was transferred to Liverpool Hospital where our youngest was born. I stayed at Alder Hey and didn't see my son for five weeks. My daughter is now 15 and doing very well, although she does find breathing difficult in certain weather. My wife is a school teacher and now lives in West Gorton.

I had a heart attack last year. I felt a totally new pain in my arm and called my older daughter who came here and made me go into hospital for a check-up. While I was there I had the heart attack. I was very lucky. I'm feeling much better now although I have good and bad days.

I have loved living on the street right from the start. I know the area well. The street has changed a lot over the years as older neighbours have moved on and new ones come. All have been friendly neighbours and still are. I love it here.

RESIDENTS IN 1911	RESIDENTS IN 2019
MACAULAY, John Born: 1844, Dublin Ireland Occupation: Late Commercial Clerk	Benny Born: 1962 Northern Ireland Occupation: Retired Kerber
MACAULAY JNR, John Born: 1879 Gymnastic Instructor	
MACAULAY, Florence Born: 1882 Manchester Lancashire Occupation: House Keeper	

Jo and Jodie

———✦———

Jo and Jodie moved to the street in 2012

Jo

Jo's Journey

We used to live a few streets away, in another part of Rusholme. We would walk through this area to Jodie's school and I thought that looked like a great place to live. While I was looking, an estate agent gave me the details of this house and I immediately fell in love with it — the style, the space — and I was delighted by the idea of having a bigger garden. As soon as I walked into the house I wanted to buy it. I'd be really sad to leave the street now; it's a special and unusual place in terms of the ways in which people interact and consciously set out to make the idea of 'community' a reality.

When I came to look at the house, I realised I already knew several people who live in the street and that also had a big appeal. I really like the fact that you can walk down the street and bump into people you know and that you can 'pop in' to see people on your doorstep. Kids from neighbouring families play out in the street and I've become close to a family from Kuwait who were living round the corner.

I love the fact that the street is very much a microcosm of Manchester. It is also both close enough to the city centre to feel part of the city — and quiet enough to feel 'tucked away'. The outlook from the house is amazing, considering we are so close to the city — large trees and gardens at the front, and our own garden at the side and back of the house. I've become more and more keen on gardening since we moved in and find it incredibly relaxing. When we moved in, the garden was a field of dandelions, and massive conifers; slowly it is becoming something more interesting.

Since moving in, I've made friends with a good number of other people in the street, primarily through the street book group that meets every six weeks or so. The group has also spurred me into reading all sorts of things I wouldn't have otherwise looked at.

I originally moved to Manchester for a job at Manchester University. I work now at Liverpool John Moores University, teaching people how to do research. I used to be a primary school teacher before doing my PhD at the University of East Anglia.

RESIDENTS IN 1911

WARNES, Walter Hawkley
Born: 1864
Manchester Lancashire
Occupation: Accountant and
Estate Agent

WARNES, Jeanie May
Born: 1878
Barrow in Furness Lancashire
Wife

WARNES, Walter Scott
Born: 1907
Manchester Lancashire

WARNES, Freda
Born: 1908
Manchester Lancashire

WARNES, William Guy
Born: 1910
Manchester Lancashire

GORST, Winifred
Born: 1896
Fenton Staffordshire
Occupation: General Servant
Domestic

RESIDENTS IN 2019

Jo
Born: 1958
Northwood, Middlesex
Occupation: Academic

Jodie
(Not pictured)
Born: 2002
North Manchester
Occupation: School Pupil

Adult Household

The original group lived on the street from July 2013,
with the latest arriving in February 2014. They left the house in 2015

Left to right: Samuel, Amy, Hannah and Laura B

Laura A's Journey

My dad worked in Chorley Hospital and my mum is a manager for a local charity in Chorley. Both have always lived in the area and I grew up there. I have three sisters and a stepsister. After secondary school in Preston I went to MMU in 2006 to do a BA Honours degree in Criminology and Sociology. I was the first person in my entire family to go to university. I had a choice of six, but chose MMU because it had the best degree. After graduation, I volunteered for a charity and very quickly was hired as a victim care officer for them. I then did a Research Master's degree in Criminology and Socio-legal Studies while working part-time. I have lived in about ten places in Manchester and moved here in February 2014 after I met Hannah through her sister (who lived in halls with me) as it seemed so much fun to live here.

Amanda's Journey

My dad immigrated to Canada from Germany as a child and my mum (who was born in Wales) came to Canada when she was 14 after living in Northern Ireland for a few years. He was studying to be a priest and my mother was also studying at the university. They met in a Latin class. When I was 3, our family moved to Dijon in France for a year and when I was 4 or 5 we returned to Vancouver in Canada for further studying at the university there. My parents separated when I was 8 and I moved to England with my mum and we lived with my great-aunt and uncle in Carlisle; Dad stayed in Canada. My mum met someone from Chorley when I was 11, so we moved there. I went to school there but dropped out of college. I met Sam and we became housemates and great friends. I worked as a care assistant and in bars until I decided to go to university at MMU in 2009 when I was 20. I graduated in 2013 with a degree in Philosophy and then got an internship with the MMU environment team and a permanent job with them a year ago. Through a gardening society at university I made some new friends and from taking a course at Hulme Garden Centre I also met Laura and we became friends. We all decided we wanted to live together in a happy place doing good things together. A group of seven of us came here in July 2013 (now five of the original seven live here and we have two new members). We saw flowers on the wall when we were house hunting and thought we want to live here. It was like a paradise.

Sam's Journey

My mum's dad (my granddad) was a miner and my mum worked in a women's refuge. My father left when I was 4. I was brought up and went to school in Coppull near Chorley. I have a twin brother and two other brothers and sisters. After school, I worked in a bar but then decided I wanted to work outside so I got an apprenticeship as a tree surgeon with a company based in Chorley. After the apprenticeship I stayed on with the company and have worked there for the past seven years. I moved here in January 2014 because I knew Amanda. Her cousin Will (one of the original seven) had moved out so I took his place.

Laura B's Journey

I lived in Maella, a small town in Zaragoza, Spain, until I was 5 years old. My dad was a veterinary surgeon but my mum stopped working when she had a family. Later, when we all grew up, she trained and became a nurse. After Maella, we moved to Caspe for a year and then to Tarazona where I grew up. I worked as a lab technician for two years before going to Zaragoza University where I studied agricultural engineering. I finished university in 2010 and then went for a three-month internship with a university in Berlin. I returned to Spain for a few months and then came to Manchester because I had a friend working here. *'Come here, it's a nice place,'* she said. I wanted to improve my English so I came. I worked in a restaurant for a couple of years but then I decided to return to Spain permanently so my parents came and got my winter clothes. Before I could return I found a job as a lab technician and because I was interested in horticulture I joined a vegetable growing and allotment course at Hulme Garden Centre – the best decision I ever made! – where there were lots of like-minded people, some from this house. A vacancy came up so I moved in and never went back to Spain after all.

Hannah's Journey

My mum was a nurse and my dad an electrician. They were both from London. I was born and brought up in Milton Keynes. I have an older brother and sister. After college I applied for university. I wanted to go to Manchester because my brother and sister were here and I liked it but I didn't get in so I went to Liverpool Hope for a year and then reapplied and did get in. I studied Leisure Tourism in Liverpool and then Tourism Management at MMU. I lived in random house shares at first but then in my second year I decided to join some societies and joined a garden society where I met Amanda and Lisa (one of our original members). We moved in together. I finished my course in July 2014, applied for an internship at MMU in marketing and promotions. I am doing that now.

Amy's Journey

My mum grew up in Chorlton before moving to Urmston and is a receptionist at Wythenshawe Hospital. My dad is from Chester and is a taxi driver. I have two younger brothers. I was brought up in Sale and attended Loreto Grammar School in Altrincham until I was 16. I went to London where I was variously a painter and decorator, estate agent and property manager. I came back to Sale when I was 20 in 2010 and did various office jobs and I am now a commercial analyst. I knew Hannah and she suggested that I move in with her and her friends. I was one of the original seven and when I came to view this house, immediately fell in love with it and the street. I love the architecture and the tiled fireplace in my bedroom. I have had a wonderful time here; the only downside was finding the boy attacked on the street last summer, which was really upsetting.

The Group

We have a lot of mice here but we don't mind. We love this street. It is a magical street. We love the way the trees are decorated at Christmas; we've been to the street party with the fire engine; have had friendly interactions with neighbours (when we needed to borrow a plunger or when collecting packages).

We've been burgled twice: one was a snatch through the window; the other was worse. The burglars pried open a rotten window when we were sleeping and stole laptops etc., and Will's car (taking the loot away in it). They were caught! Our neighbours were very supportive.

We still love it here. We love the children on the street. We've got lots of bikes here and don't add to the car problem!

Amy (in August 2015): Later this month the household is breaking up, with up to four of us going to Copenhagen to study where there are no tuition fees. The rest of us, including myself, are moving elsewhere in Manchester. We are really sad to go, although it is exciting too. We have loved living here. It's the end of an era.

RESIDENTS IN 1911

CARTWRIGHT, Stanley
Born: 1875
Tunstall Staffordshire
Occupation: Accountant Clerk

CARTWRIGHT, Gertrude
Born: 1880
Middleborough Yorkshire
Wife

BROUGHTON, Martha
Born: 1888
Newton Le Willows Lancashire
Occupation: General Servant
Domestic

RESIDENTS IN 2015

Samuel
Born: 1988
Preston
Occupation: Tree Surgeon

Amy
Born: 1990
Urmston
Occupation: Commercial
Analyst

Hannah
Born: 1990
Milton Keynes
Occupation: Marketing and
Promotions Intern, Manchester
Metropolitan University

Laura B
Born: 1984
Zaragoza, Spain
Occupation: Laboratory
Technician

Laura A
(Not pictured)
Born: 1988
Preston, Lancashire
Occupation: Victim Care Officer

Amanda
(Not pictured)
Born: 1988
Edmonton, Canada
Occupation: Sustainability
Engagement Officer,
Manchester Metropolitan
University

**Andrew (not pictured or
present for inteview)**

The authors would like to thank:

All our neighbours, for their active contribution to life on our street, their stories and for making this project possible. Special thanks are due to Harry Spooner, who first shared the 1911 Census with us, Helen Glaizner and Nicky Johnson, who worked with us on a book for Manchester primary schools based on this project, and Sue Morgan and Elizabeth Parish for valuable editorial assistance.

Our three local councillors – Rabnawaz Akbar, Jill Lovecy and Ahmed Ali – who have championed our residents' group and this project throughout and who have facilitated Manchester City Council's support for this book.

David, Dennis, Leo, Renate and the congregation of the New Apostolic Church ,who have supported our residents' association and this project by willingly offering accommodation and a welcome.

Committee members of our residents' association, who have freely given their time and energy to the community and for backing this project.

Jackie Ould and the Ahmed Iqbal Ullah Education Trust, who supported the production of a version of this story for Manchester Primary Schools, and Manchester Central Library for hosting a touch screen version of the project.

The History Press and Nicola Guy, for having faith in our project and publishing *Stories from a Manchester Street*.

Elaine's Thursday Writing Group, for their continued interest and advice from the very first interview to the last.

Helena Kettleborough, Phil's civil partner and Elaine's steadfast friend, for her unstinting support, encouragement and enthusiasm past, present and future.

The History Press

The destination for history
www.thehistorypress.co.uk